D0609343

meredith
andrea
phillips

The Private Lives of
ORCHIDS

The Private Lives of

J. B. Lippincott Company

ORCHIDS

Written and Illustrated by

Hilda Simon

PHILADELPHIA and NEW YORK

Copyright © 1975 by Hilda Simon

All Rights Reserved
First Edition

Printed in the United States of America

U.S. Library of Congress Cataloging in Publication Data

Simon, Hilda.
  The private lives of orchids.

  1. Orchids. I. Title.
QK495.O64S56   584′.15   74–18331
ISBN–0–397–01075–3

To Beatrice Rosenfeld

in gratitude

for her friendship, encouragement, and cooperation

Contents

The Mysterious Orchid   13

The Anatomy of the Orchid   33

Orchids and Their Pollinators   53

A Showcase of Tropical Orchids   75

Orchids of the Temperate Zones   99

Mimics, Masks, and Other Oddities   125

Geographical Ranges of Orchids   147

Bibliography   154

Index   155

Illustrations

A pink variety of the South American *Laelia purpurata*   Frontispiece

Sphinx Moth pollinating the Star-of-Bethlehem Orchid of
    Madagascar   12

A *Cattleya* orchid commonly used in corsages   16

Paphinia grandiflora of Brazil   17

A typical member of the genus *Orchis*   18

Paired tuberous roots of all *Orchis* species   19

A spectrum of blossom shapes found in orchids   22–23

Many orchids have minute flowers   24

Giant blossoms, such as this cattleya, are common among orchid
    species   25

A spectrum of colors found in orchids   26–27

A typical terrestrial orchid   29

A typical epiphytic orchid   30

Monopodial orchid with seed capsules and flowers   32

Sympodial orchid with pseudobulbs   34

An orchid with flowers as wide as the plant is high   35

A single blossom of the Bamboo Orchid   36

The Bamboo Orchid   37

Male and female flowers of a *Cycnoches* species   38

Modifications of the labellum, or lip, in various species   39

The European *Loroglossum hirzium*, with a greatly modified lip   40

Parts of an orchid flower   41

An orchid with upright flowers   42

An orchid with hanging flowers   43

Cycnoches chlorochilon   45
Typical orchid seeds and the atypical vanilla seed   46
A commercially important *Vanilla* species   47
Diagram of an orchid protocorm   48
Stanhopea wardii   50
Euglossid bees visiting a *Catasetum* orchid   52
Hummingbird pollinating a South American orchid   54–55
Swallowtail butterfly visiting an *Epidendrum* species   56–57
Extreme sexual dimorphism in a *Catasetum* species   59
A *Bulbophyllum* species that has small, ill-smelling flowers   61
Pollination of an orchid, with a portion of the flower shown in
    cross-section   62
The wishbone antennae in a *Catasetum* flower   63
Diagram of a Trapdoor Orchid   65
Diagram of a Bucket Orchid   66
Southern European *Ophrys* species with visiting bees   68–69
Blossoms of three different *Ophrys* species   70
Phalaenopsis amabilis, a lovely tropical orchid found in the
    Himalayas   72–73
A handsome member of the *Cattleya* genus   74
A typical unifoliate cattleya   79
A typical bifoliate cattleya   80
Cattleya forbesii   81
Cattleya guttata   82
Guatemala's Flor de Jesus, *Laelia rubescens*   83
The well-known Cockleshell Orchid   84
Odontoglossum crispum   85
The Tiger Orchid   86
The Butterfly Orchid of the genus *Oncidium*   87
Paphiopedilum insigne, an Asiatic Lady's Slipper   89
Dendrobium fimbriatum, found at high altitudes in the Himalayas   90
Coelogyne cristata of the Himalayas   91
The Himalayan *Vanda coerulea*, one of the rare blue orchids   93
Cymbidium hookerianum, an Asiatic species   94
Disa graminifolia, a blue orchid found in Africa   95
An *Aeranthes* species of Madagascar   96
The European Bee Orchid, *Ophrys apifera*   98
Orchis morio, a typical terrestrial orchid   101
Orchis palustris, the European Swamp Orchid   102
Nigritella nigra, a European mountain orchid   103

The Bird's Nest Orchid 105

The most distinctive feature of *Corallorhiza* is its root system 106

The Glass Orchid 107

The flowers of *Spiranthes aestivalis* face in every direction 108

A flower of the European Lady's Slipper 109

Three *Cypripedium* species 110

Calypso bulbosa, the sole representative of an entire genus 113

Single blossoms of five European *Orchis* species 114

European Butterfly Orchid of the genus *Orchis* 115

Two color varieties of a *Dactylorhiza* species 116

Orchis spectabilis, the Showy Orchid 117

Single flower of the North American Yellow Fringed Orchid 118

Ophrys hybrids 119

An attractive *Ophrys* species 120

The Grass Orchid, *Calopogon pulchellus* 121

Bletilla striata of the Far East and *Pogonia ophiogolossoides,* the Bearded Orchid of North America 122

The Bucket Orchid 124

A Swan Orchid of the genus *Cycnoches* 126

Ophrys blossoms and the insects they supposedly mimic 127

India's Leaf Butterfly, an accomplished mimic of dry leaves 128

The Malaysian Orchid Mantis 129

The Scorpion Orchid 130

Holy Ghost Orchid 131

Single flower of the European Doll Orchid 132

The weird flower of the Hammer Orchid 133

Rhizanthella, the unique subterranean orchid of Australia 134

Flowers and buds of *Grammatophyllum speciosum* 135

A dwarf Lady's Slipper 136

A miniature orchid of tropical America 137

A South American Lady's Slipper with extremely long petals 138

A *Brassia* species with greatly elongated sepals 139

The Cucumber Orchid 140

The Braided Orchid 141

The leafless Ghost Orchid 142

Dendrobium phalaenopsis of New Guinea 144

Crestless Gardener Bowerbird with a *Dendrobium* blossom in its beak 145

Graphic guide to world-wide distribution of important or familiar genera 148–53

The Mysterious Orchid

MORE THAN A CENTURY AGO, a large, showy orchid found in Madagascar aroused the interest of botanists studying these plants. Its star-shaped, milk-white, heavily scented flowers measured almost seven inches across and seemed to glow against the background of lush, dark-green foliage. The shape of this striking orchid and the fact that it usually blooms around Christmastime determined the choice of one of its popular names: the Star of Bethlehem.

It was not, however, the size or beauty of this orchid that intrigued the botanists, but the puzzling inaccessibility of the nectary, which was at the very bottom of the narrow, almost-foot-long nectar tube, or spur, that extended downward from the flower. How could any insect capable of pollinating the orchid possibly reach the nectar? And yet it was clear that the flower, like most orchids, had to depend upon cross-pollinization.

In the early 1860's, Charles Darwin came across this puzzle and proposed its solution: the pollinator had to be an insect, most likely a moth, with a proboscis long enough to reach down to the nectar in the tube. But such an insect was not known to biologists; nor was one discovered in the four decades that followed. In 1891, when expectations of finding such an insect had been largely dissipated, Alfred Russel Wallace, a contemporary and friend of Darwin, revived and elaborated upon his famous colleague's prediction. Wallace asserted that the insect pollinator of the Star-of-Bethlehem Orchid would prove to be a member of a cosmopolitan family of large, long-tongued lepidoptera known as Hawk, or Sphinx, Moths. Twelve years later, in 1903, the freshly inspired search for the hypothetical night flier yielded results: a hawk moth with a proboscis eleven inches long was found on Madagascar. Although it never had actually been observed feeding from the orchid, there was no doubt that the Star of Bethlehem's elusive pollinator—which received the eminently suitable species name *praedicta*—had finally been discovered.

The curious facts Darwin learned in his studies of orchids and their fertilization so astonished and fascinated him that he wrote a two-volume work, entitled *The Various Contrivances by Which Orchids Are Fertilised by Insects,* which later became a classic.

In the late nineteenth century, wealthy Europeans, predominantly members of the English nobility, paid thousands of dollars for a single new rare and unusual orchid plant from the tropical jungles. During the height of the European orchid craze, these flowers became synonymous with the strange, the exotic, and the mysterious. The blooming of an unusual tropical species in a greenhouse of England, Holland, or Germany was a newsworthy item throughout Europe. English import firms especially vied with each other in obtaining the greatest number of new varieties. Orchid hunting was such a lucrative enterprise that, at the apex of that era, a single English firm employed at least one hundred and forty orchid hunters. These adventurous seekers after the living gold of the tropics risked—and frequently lost—their lives in the cloud forests of South America and the jungles of Madagascar and New Guinea. They traveled on foot and by canoe, they fought their way up the Amazon and the Orinoco, and they braved tropical fevers, venomous snakes, the poisoned arrows of hostile natives, and the voracious piranhas dwelling in the South American streams near which so many of the most prized orchids occur.

Even after they sighted the objects of their search, they faced the problem of getting at the plants, most of which grew in tall trees, sometimes at inaccessible heights of sixty, eighty, or a hundred feet above the ground. Although it has been said that some hunters, unable to climb the trees to the height of the plants, even tried training monkeys to bring them down, most often the trees were felled. This was no simple task either, in the "green hell" of the jungle with its maze of lianas and other vegetation— apart from the danger of damaging the very plants the hunters were after. Then, when the quarry was finally secured and carefully packed, came the long boat trip home, during which many prize plants either died or bloomed prematurely.

But even if the hunter arrived with just a few rare and beautiful new orchid species, he was paid handsomely, besides becoming a hero in the eyes of those romantics to whom his quest embodied the thrill of danger and mystery.

Since the turn of the century, so much knowledge has been accumulated about orchids and their life cycle, so many exotic species have been raised in greenhouses, that the majority can now be grown domestically by those who want to spend the necessary time, money, and effort. If it is considered essential to obtain a plant from the wild—and in most countries where indigenous orchids occur, such collecting is strictly regulated today by the respective governments to prevent abuse—the expeditions are handled with the help of helicopters that can be set down in formerly inaccessible places.

No longer a "craze," the interest of people in orchids has not only persisted but has spread widely on a more informed level.

A Cattleya *orchid commonly used in corsages.*

Orchid societies in many countries are devoted to the study, raising, and breeding of orchids, and especially to the creation of new varieties by artificial hybridization. The American Orchid Society has some 15,000 members and 270 affiliated regional groups that regularly exchange information with their counterparts in other countries and publish a number of orchid periodicals. Moreover, commercial growers have made many species of orchids familiar to the average flower buyer, bringing the orchid corsage within the reach of even the thrifty. And yet there still clings to this flower the aura of luxury, glamor, and the special occasion.

Not only florists' customers but those of us who have seen a variety of orchids displayed at flower shows may think we have at least a general idea of what orchids "look like," and yet for every flower that most people could easily identify as an orchid,

Paphinia grandiflora *of Brazil.*

there are literally thousands of other species they would be quite unable to recognize; for the truth is that there is simply no such thing as a "typical" orchid, at least as far as appearance is concerned. Of all the flowering plants on earth, no other group can match the incredible diversity and variability of the orchid family.

What common denominator could possibly bind together this bewildering array of seemingly unrelated plants? It is the structure of the flower—though its essential details are not always easy to distinguish, even for a knowledgeable layman, such are its intricacies and its many individual variations and modifications.

Most of these will be discussed in the next chapter, but it should be mentioned here that it was not the structure of the flower, nor of any normally visible plant part, that gave the

A typical member of the genus Orchis.

orchid family its botanical name, Orchidaceae. And it is rather ironic that, although the word "orchid" usually brings to mind the more spectacular tropical species, the family name originated from a feature found only in certain terrestrial orchids of the temperate latitudes.

The orchids of the temperate zones all have tuberous roots of varying shapes in which moisture and nutrients are stored; and from these underground storehouses, which are well protected against freezing temperatures, new growth issues each spring. The members of the genus *Orchis*—widespread throughout Europe—usually have roundish, paired tubers. Nineteen hundred years ago Pedanius Dioscorides, a Greek medical writer of the first century, was struck by the peculiar shape of the tubers, which reminded him of the male genital glands. He accordingly named the plant *orchis,* which is Greek for "testicle," and later this name was applied not only to that one genus as *Orchis,* but to the entire family, both scientifically as Orchidaceae and popularly in many languages, including our own English "orchid," even though the majority of orchids do not have this

Paired tuberous roots (shown enlarged) of an Orchis *species.*

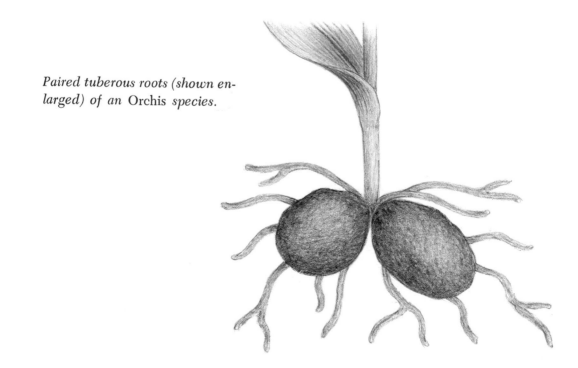

kind of root. The type genus *Orchis* has representatives not only in Europe but also in North America and temperate Asia; in Germany, these orchids are popularly known as *Knabenkraut*—"boy's herb"—because the tubers, dried and pulverized, were formerly credited with being a powerful aphrodisiac and were used in love potions. Needless to say, they lack any such properties; it was lucky for those who swallowed the concoctions that the roots are not poisonous. Later, in fact, because of their gelatinous nature, they were found to alleviate such conditions as croup and diarrhea, and preparations made of the tubers were sold under the trade name of Salep until more effective aids for these disorders became available and largely replaced them.

Actually, considering the thousands of different orchid species, it seems odd that there should not be any with distinctive medicinal properties among them; so far, however, none has been discovered. On the contrary, the huge family is curiously lacking in economically important species—with the notable exception of the unique vanilla orchid, about which more will be said later. Even allowing for those species used commercially for corsages and other ornamental purposes, the extensive attraction of orchids for people is certainly not primarily economic or material, but ranges from a purely esthetic appeal to the spell of the exotic and unusual.

Comprising at least 25,000 species, orchids are the largest family of flowering plants in the world; and the unparalleled diversity of its individual members mentioned earlier includes not only such physical features as sizes, shapes, and colors but life styles, habitats, and environments. Although commonly assumed to be products of the tropical and subtropical climates, orchids in fact occur in practically all parts of the world, with the exception only of the desert and polar regions. The temperate zones of every continent, even in the northern latitudes, can all boast of their indigenous species, although these usually have relatively small and inconspicuous blossoms.

The dizzying multiplicity of orchids as well as their great adaptability and variability have led to the evolution of "specialists" that are suited for almost any type of climate and environment. Some orchids, for instance, have developed means of living high up in the branches of tropical trees without any soil to nourish their root systems, while others can survive in the woods of temperate regions and the permanent semishade of the forest floor. Some orchids prefer wet meadows, swamps, and bogs; others, dry, rocky ground, sand dunes, and open sunny locations. Certain orchids are found in the mountain ranges of the Alps, the Andes, and the Himalayas, at altitudes ranging upward to 14,000 feet, where the climate is harsh and cold and few other blooming plants occur. At least one kind of orchid is semiaquatic, lifting only its flowers above the water surface, while another species is completely subterranean, growing and blooming year after year hidden away underground.

By their very nature, some of these highly specialized orchids are narrowly confined to a certain ecological niche, and if the balance of such an environment is altered even slightly, the orchid is immediately endangered. Other, less specialized species are also less vulnerable. Some terrestrial orchids have a relatively wide range of habitats, occurring in woods, in swamps and meadows, and on mountain slopes at various altitudes.

In regard to size, color, shape, and even smell, it seems as though Nature has given the orchid family the green light for runaway diversity. Beginning with the size of the plants, one species may grow to a height of twenty-five feet, while at the other extreme there are midgets only a fraction of an inch high. The leaves, although they all share the basic feature of parallel leaf veins, may be elongate or roundish, thin and paperlike, or thick and fleshy. Some orchids look like reeds or bamboo grasses; others resemble cactus growths. Although most species have relatively few leaves, some have such thick and dense foliage that they are used as hedges—and then again, some have no leaves

Some familiar blossom shapes, typical of many orchid groups. (All orchids on this and the opposite page are shown in monotone to accentuate variation in shape.)

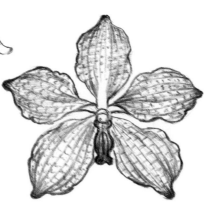

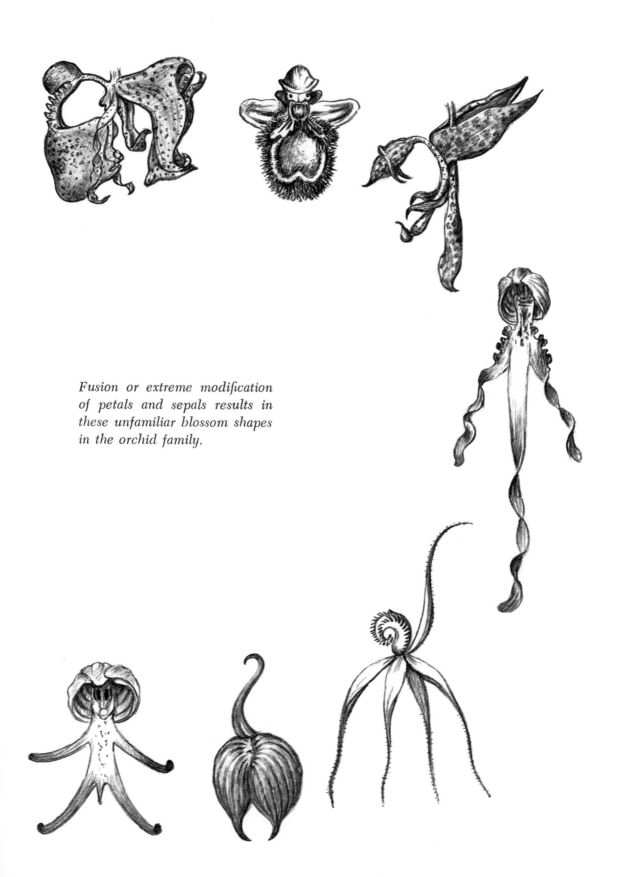

Fusion or extreme modification of petals and sepals results in these unfamiliar blossom shapes in the orchid family.

at all, bringing forth only flowers on an otherwise bare stem.

Similarly, the flowers may grow singly on a stem or grouped into clusters of up to several dozen blossoms. Orchids may be shaped like cups, helmets, buckets, caps, or shoes; their sepals and petals may be modified to form tubes, tendrils, ribbons, or taillike appendages. They may be smooth, hairy, ruffled, fringed, or toothed. Some are delicate and tissue-thin, others thick and solid with a waxy or even leathery texture. There are giants that measure ten inches across and dwarfs with a flower no larger than a pinhead.

In line with the enormous number of orchid species that a single genus may include—some genera have more than a thousand species—a large percentage of species display a tendency to extensive natural hybridization, and thus to a proliferation of new variants. Deciding whether a newly discovered orchid is in fact a new species or only a subspecies or variant of an already known kind is frequently a difficult problem for the experts. This accounts for the many discrepancies that appear in the numbers of species acknowledged by different authorities, although a minimum of 25,000 seems to have been established. This number does not, of course, include the thousands of orchid hybrids bred artificially by professional and amateur growers. Establishing such new orchid types is strictly regulated; to be officially acknowledged, a hybrid must be registered with the Royal Horticultural Society of England, whose list is internationally recognized.

Many orchids have minute flowers.

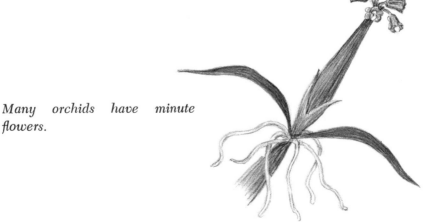

Giant blossoms, such as this cattleya, are common among orchid species.

The spectrum of colors found in orchids includes white, lavender, and a wide range of pinks.

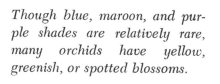

Though blue, maroon, and purple shades are relatively rare, many orchids have yellow, greenish, or spotted blossoms.

The popular notion that orchids are always tropical flowers, though erroneous, is understandable; for not only the greatest number but also the largest, showiest, most beautiful, and most bizarre species are found in the tropical and subtropical regions of the world, especially in South America, Madagascar, and the Malayan Archipelago. There bloom the orchids with flowers as much as eight or ten inches across; there one can find plants bearing as many as thirty four-inch blossoms on a single flower spike that forms a breath-taking spectacle of beauty; and there prevail the vivid pinks, lavenders, reds, and golden-yellows and the fantastic shapes and forms.

Especially eye-catching is the rich assortment of colors and patterns. Every conceivable hue from pure white to almost blackish purple is to be found among orchids—even though the legendary "black orchid," like the black rose, is only a figment of the imagination, or at least an unfulfilled dream of orchid growers. None of the chromatic colors, however, are missing from the spectrum of orchid shades—there are pinks and reds and yellows, blues and browns and greens, lavender and orange and ivory and purple. Blossoms may be solid-colored or multicolored, speckled, barred, striped, streaked, or blotched.

Similarly, the smells emitted by the various orchid species range from the most delicate and pleasant fragrances to the offensive odors of decay and putrid flesh. In addition to the vanilla orchid, from which we get the popular flavoring, many other orchids have a similar vanillalike scent. There are species that smell like ripe bananas or other fruits; and still others that have their own individual fragrances, unlike any other scent. There are also a number of orchids that have no scent at all.

It must be plain by now that no one orchid or orchid type could possibly be truly representative of a plant family of such staggering variety. However, the genus *Cattleya*—so named in honor of the English botanist and orchid fancier James Cattley— is commonly considered the queen of the orchids, and some of its species have become the best-known and commercially most successful, so much so, in fact, that to many people the large and showy *Cattleya* orchids have become the prototypes of *the* orchid. This is somewhat regrettable because thousands of other species that are perhaps even more beautiful, though less spectacular than the cattleyas, deserve their full share of attention.

The orchid family can be roughly divided into two large

A typical terrestrial orchid: a Lady's Slipper.

A *typical epiphytic orchid:*
Bulbophyllum longifolium.

groups: the terrestrial species and the epiphytic—those which grow perched on trees without any soil base. The first includes all those found in temperate zones; the second, most of the tropical orchids. For although terrestrial and semiterrestrial species are found in the tropics, no epiphytic orchids occur naturally in the temperate regions: obviously climates in which the temperatures sink below the freezing point cannot accommodate plants that must live without root protection.

Even though the epiphytic orchids do not have to survive inclement weather, they, like all living organisms, are faced with a number of problems in their struggle for existence.

What these problems are and how the epiphytes cope with them and thrive will be described in a later chapter. Meantime, we shall next look at the structure of orchids in general and, in particular, at some of the amazing intricacies of their means of reproduction.

The Anatomy of the Orchid

AT FIRST GLANCE, it would appear almost impossible to find and describe, among the many thousands of orchid varieties, the common structural features that establish all of them as members of the same family. Over the years, the patience and perseverance of botanists from many countries have succeeded in sorting out and identifying this bewildering and confusing array, in locating and defining the similarities and common denominators among the many differences, deviations, and modifications of structure that distinguish the orchid family.

Botanists classify orchids as monocots—which is short for monocotyledons—as opposed to dicots, or dicotyledons. These formidable-sounding words mean simply single- and double-leafed, respectively, a cotyledon being the very first leaf that is formed by the seedling—usually very different from the later, typical leaves of a plant. Bananas, palms, grasses, lilies, and orchids have only a single cotyledon, whereas herbs, shrubs, and most deciduous trees have two.

In addition to the extreme differences in the flowers, leaves, and general plant structure of the orchids, their growth patterns also vary considerably. According to these, botanists distinguish two main groups of orchids as the sympodial and the monopodial.

*Sympodial orchid with pseudobulbs
in different growth stages.*

Sympodial orchids have a main stem that stops growing at the end of each season; the flowers are the final product of that stem. In the next season, a new lead branch forms at the base of the plant and develops into a stem which eventually will produce flowers. An often greatly thickened stem called a pseudobulb is a distinctive feature of most sympodial orchids of the tropics.

The monopodial species follow an entirely different growth pattern. The stem continues to grow steadily year after year. The flowers—usually several, and frequently arranged in sprays—grow from stalks between the leaves.

These differences in growth patterns as well as in the number, size, shape, and arrangement of the leaves add up to great variations in the appearance of different orchid plants, which may be short or tall, thin and reedlike or squat and chunky, practically leafless or multileaved. The Bamboo Orchid of the Himalayas and Malaysia, often grown as a hedge, attains a height of eight feet and has only a few flowers at the tips of stems

An orchid with flowers as wide as the plant is high.

A single blossom of the Bamboo Orchid (shown at right).

bearing dozens of leaves, and some other species grow even taller. In all these orchids, the flower is relatively small compared to the leaves and stalks; a six-foot African species, for instance, has two-foot leaves but flowers that measure only three inches across. Among other types of orchids, the flowers are frequently as large as the leaves, or even larger—so much so in some species that the plants appear top-heavy.

Despite these differences in plant size, appearance, and growth pattern, the basic flower structure that distinguishes all orchids follows a pattern of threes. There are three leaves called sepals that form the outer whorl, and three petals forming the inner whorl. These six flower leaves are present in all orchids, although they may often be so reduced, fused, or otherwise modified that they are difficult to identify except by an expert.

In most other flowers the outer whorl, whose leaves have the function of protecting the bud, consists of usually greenish sepals that are thicker and tougher than the more delicate, colored petals of the inner whorl. Not so the orchids: their sepals are just as colorful as the petals, and typically similar in texture. Together, the six leaves form a symmetrical flower arrangement,

in which the central sepal and the central petal—which are located opposite each other—usually have a shape that differs from that of the other two pairs. The middle sepal is frequently modified to form a caplike or helmetlike structure, while the middle petal is the "display" portion of the flower—generally the largest and most colorful of the six leaves. This petal—the "lip," or labellum—is subject to an unimaginable variety of modifications in the various orchid species. Only in those species that rely mainly on their fragrance for attracting the insects they need for pollination do we find instances of inconspicuous lip structure and coloration.

The smallest, usually least visible, but most important parts of the flower are the reproductive organs located at its center. Like many other plants, orchids as a rule have bisexual flowers, although some species not only have separate male and female blossoms, but also grow them on different plants! This has caused considerable confusion among botanists, for the male and female flowers of some orchids look so different that they were erroneously classified as separate species before the connection was established.

Male and female flowers of a Cycnoches *species.*

Modifications of the labellum, or lip, in various species.

In the bisexual flowers, however, the fleshy, club-shaped column, a fusion of male and female reproductive organs, projects from the center of the blossom. At the base, the column is fused to the ovary, which before fertilization looks like a part of the flower stem.

At the very top of the column is the male organ called the anther, which contains the pollen. In contrast to the familiar yellow pollen dust of most other flowers, the individual pollen grains of practically all orchids are gathered in a coherent mass, the pollinium, with the help of a viscous substance that binds thousands of them together into what looks like a tiny club. Each anther bears two or more of these pollinia, and each pollinium is held to the base at its thin end by a sticky, glandlike body. Consisting of the same viscous mass that envelops the pollen

The European Loroglossum hirzium, *showing its greatly modified lip.*

Color code

Petals: dark pink
Sepals: light pink
Lip: light pink, spotted
Stigma: green
Nectary entrance: brown

Parts of an orchid flower.

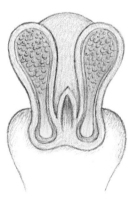

Color code

Anther: light green
Pollinia: yellow

Anther of an orchid flower.

grains, the base of the pollinium adheres easily to the body of a visiting insect, which pulls out and carries off the pollen packets as it comes into contact with the anther.

Directly below the anther is the female organ, the stigma, with a depressed and equally sticky surface, on which a pollinium must be deposited in order to fertilize the flower. Despite the close proximity of the male and female organs, the mechanism of

In orchids with upright flowers, the ovaries revolve through a 180-degree angle so that the lips face downward.

In orchids with hanging flowers, the lips naturally extend downward.

pollination is so arranged in practically all orchids as to prevent fertilization of a flower by its own pollen. To insure cross-pollination, the pollen packet must be brought into just the right spot for adhering to the stigma of the next orchid visited by the insect; the erect posture of the pollinium on the insect's body must be altered. This occurs when the insect leaves the flower and the thin membrane that forms the stem of the club shrinks upon exposure to the air. As the stem shrinks, the head of the club is forced to bend forward and down.

One of the most interesting habits of most orchid flowers is the maneuver enacted by the ovary just before the flower opens. At that time, the stemlike ovary executes a 180-degree turn, reversing the location of the labellum and the middle sepal. The uppermost part of the flower now becomes the lower part, so that the conspicuous lip faces downward—becoming an alluring advertising piece—the ideal landing strip for insect pollinators!

Among certain epiphytic species, we find a most logical exception to this maneuver: although most of these orchids have lips that face downward, only those that bear their flowers on erect stems turn them around, whereas those that produce blossoms on hanging or drooping spikes do not, for if they did, the lips would be the uppermost part of the hanging flower, whose position is naturally upside down. One thing that led some orchid fanciers to the extravagant claim that orchids can think was the behavior of hanging flowers when botanists experimentally forced them into an upright position by tying their spikes to stakes. Within twenty-four hours, their ovaries had executed the 180-degree turn necessary to make the lip of every flower face downward again!

The main function of all the attention-getting shapes, colors, and scents of orchid blossoms, as well as the peculiar arrangements of their reproductive parts, is of course the attraction of insects and other animals capable of fertilizing the flowers. So variously complex and occasionally "devious" are the means and apparatus developed by orchids to entice and even trick the pollinators into fulfilling their vital role that the next chapter will be entirely devoted to what Darwin so aptly called these contrivances. For the present, we shall assume that fertilization has been successfully completed, that the ovary has turned into a seed capsule filled with ripe seeds, and that new life can begin.

An orchid seed pod or capsule normally contains a tremendous number of minute seeds, often as fine as powder. The record for the greatest number of seeds belongs to the tropical species *Cycnoches chlorochilon,* a handsome orchid with large yellow flowers. An effort to count the individual seeds in a single capsule yielded the staggering number of 3,770,000. The genus *Cycnoches,* popularly known as the Swan Orchid, is remarkable for several other interesting features. The lip generally

Cycnoches chlorochilon, *distinguished for having almost four million seeds in a single capsule.*

points upward, and the long, curved column—which suggested the name—is completely exposed. Several species in this group may have both male and female flowers at different times on the same plant. Some species produce predominantly male flowers, others are bisexual. Propagation in this group is as often vegetative—through offshoots—as through seeds.

The fineness and lightness of the orchid seeds—those almost four million *Cycnoches* seeds weigh about half an ounce—makes them easy for the wind to carry. Even the slightest breeze can waft along the tiny granules, scattering them over a wide area. The majority go to waste, because they do not find a suitable spot for germination, and even those that do may remain seemingly lifeless and inactive for a period of several months before they begin to take root. This ability is related to their unusually high fat content, which prevents easy absorption of moisture and stands the seeds in good stead if they have to wait for prime conditions for germination, because they can lie for years without rotting even in moist locations.

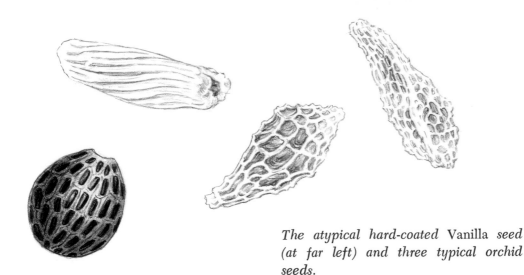

The atypical hard-coated Vanilla *seed (at far left) and three typical orchid seeds.*

Orchid seeds are not, however, at all well equipped for independence from outside food sources during the first crucial period of development. Compared to the richly nutritive "envelope" with which the seed of other plants is surrounded and from which the plant embryo can sustain itself, the minute quantities of nutrients in the typical orchid seed are negligible. We have to think only of such seeds as grains and nuts, beans and peas and lentils, to realize how widespread and generous this provision for most plant embryos is in nature—so generous, in fact, that countless animals, including man, use them for food. In the case of the orchid seeds, the advantages of independent sources of nutrition have been sacrificed for those of smallness and lightness. It is evidently vital to the orchids that their seeds can be carried easily by the wind and can be spread over a wide area, probably because locations suitable for orchid growth are few and far between. This is obvious in the case of the epiphytic orchids that have to establish themselves in tiny crevices in the bark of trees where there is no soil base, and where survival is precarious even under otherwise good conditions.

On the other hand, the seeds of the vanilla orchids are quite atypical. The genus *Vanilla* includes about sixty-five species that occur widely throughout tropical America. They are climbing orchids whose vines may attain a length of fifty feet. As they wind themselves around the trunks of supporting trees, their fleshy stems put out many air roots. *Vanilla planifolia,* the economically most important species, is native to the coastal forests of Mexico. Its long seed pods are harvested when still not ripe; vanillin, the fragrant constituent of vanilla flavoring, is obtained through a fermenting process.

The seeds of the *Vanilla* species are relatively large, and, instead of the transparent seed coat that encloses the average orchid embryo, they have a hard outer coating which has to decay to permit germination of the embryo. The economic importance and the unusual seed structures of the vanilla orchids have invested them with an interest which their inconspicuous green flowers would not have inspired.

One of the commercially important Vanilla *species.*

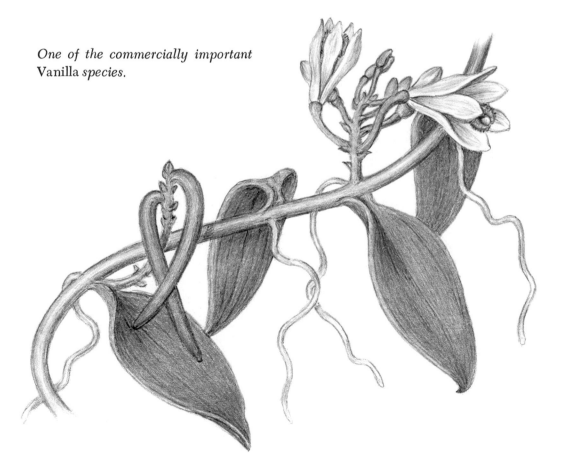

Unlike the vanilla embryo, the average orchid embryo—whether epiphytic or terrestrial—must, of course, be capable of somehow compensating for the lack of nutrients in the seed. It manages to do so by relying on factors that were discovered only after lengthy studies. The most important—and truly astonishing—of these factors is the delicately balanced symbiotic relationship with certain funguses, one of the most unusual between different organisms known to man. The unique and intriguing fact about this peculiar symbiosis is that it does not start out at all as a mutually beneficial association. On the contrary, the fungus—which varies with various orchid species—initially seeks out the seed to attack it and feed upon its pathetically small oil and protein reserves. In some mysterious fashion, the seedling soon begins a counterattack and starts to digest portions of the fungus intruder. Within a short time, the attacked has turned into the attacker, for the orchid embryo becomes a parasite and, for a while, lives altogether off the fungus.

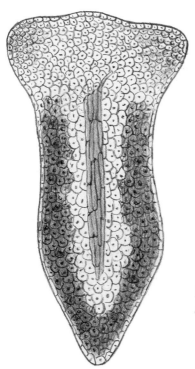

Color code

Orchid embryo: green
Portions on which fungus feeds: brown

Diagram of an orchid protocorm, greatly enlarged.

Now all depends upon whether a balance can be struck between the two adversaries that will turn them into partners. If the fungus is too strong, it will destroy the seedling and absorb it; should the seedling prove too strong, it will digest the fungus completely—and with it, kill off its own means of survival. Usually—and miraculously—a precarious balance is established, with the fungus living in and off the outer tissue of the orchid embryo, while the seedling digests those portions of the fungus that extend into its interior. This complicated equilibrium is made even more precarious by the fact that only the "right" kind of fungus will do for any particular orchid species; if a "wrong" fungus is attracted by the chemical substances of the seed—and this does occur sometimes—the developing orchid is doomed.

If all goes well, a bulb-shaped body called the protocorm is formed, containing the elements for a root system and the plant stem. In this protocorm, the fungus can live and feed while at the same time being fed upon by the young orchid plant. Even in the rhizomes—the rootlike underground stems of many terrestrial orchids—funguses often occur, but not in their underground tubers, which are food-storage units that function independently.

Closely connected with the dependence of the orchids upon a symbiotic relationship with the "food" funguses is their extreme sensitivity to changes in the ecology of their environment. Should the composition of the soil be altered—through introduction of chemical fertilizers, for example, or heavy levels of weed killers or insecticides—the orchid fungus can no longer survive, and without it, the orchid also dies.

If everything goes well, the orchid continues to grow and, finally, to bloom. The development from seed to flowering plant is a very lengthy process, usually taking several years. Some *Orchis* species do not bloom until six to nine years after germination, but another genus, *Cypripedium,* probably holds the record: the most famous of terrestrial orchids, the Lady's Slipper, needs from fifteen to seventeen years to bring forth its first flower!

It is clear from such examples that, in order to bloom at all, orchids generally have to be long-lived plants. Furthermore, the first flowers are apt to be only the beginning of a life span that is far out of proportion to the plant's size; and indeed, some tropical orchids are known to have a life expectancy similar to that of man. There are instances of orchid plants that have been passed on from one generation to another, as in Miami's Orchid Jungle, where the grandson cared for the very plants collected by his grandfather decades earlier.

This longevity applies not only to the plants themselves, but also to the flowers. The blossoms of most orchids last longer than practically any other type of flower—unless they are fertilized. Once fertilization occurs, the blossoms wilt very quickly, probably through the influence of certain substances activated by the pollen as soon as it becomes embedded in the stigma. In any case, only unfertilized orchids can be kept fresh for any length of time —several weeks in some cases—which is why orchid growers who

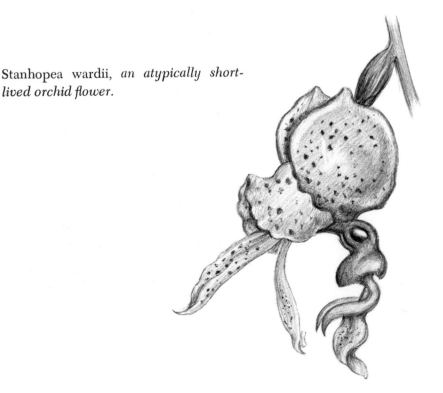

Stanhopea wardii, *an atypically short-lived orchid flower.*

sell their flowers commercially are anxious to prevent any possibility of pollination.

Of course, orchids would not be orchids if there were no exceptions to this general rule of flower longevity. Certain species, such as the strange-looking Mexican orchid *Stanhopea wardii*, have blossoms that open so quickly that one can watch the process of unfolding. Unfortunately, even the unfertilized blossoms wilt just as quickly, lasting only twenty-four hours.

Before they begin to bloom, many orchids enter into a resting period, in which the growth process all but stops. During that time the pseudobulbs become dry and shriveled, and the entire plant is a rather sorry sight. Nevertheless, this rest period is absolutely necessary for the orchid if it later is to produce fine, strong flowers. Growers of tropical orchids have learned this through long experience, just as they have learned that there are certain "orchid years" during which the plants produce an especially lush crop of flowers and other years when they hardly bloom at all. This peculiarity also applies to the terrestrial orchids of temperate zones, which occasionally skip a year and then bloom again the following spring or summer, thus confirming the orchids' reputation for unpredictability and individualism.

Orchids and Their Pollinators

EVEN TAKING INTO ACCOUNT the great variety mentioned earlier of the orchid family's pollination systems, most of them have one thing in common: with the exception of about 3 percent of known orchid species that have evolved a mechanism for self-pollination, all orchids are dependent upon animals—usually insects—for fertilization of the flowers. Hence each genus has developed both the appropriate means for attracting the individual insect or insects capable of achieving its pollination and the precise mechanism designed to prevent the visitor from leaving without fulfilling its vital role in the life cycle of the plant.

As one looks incredulously at some of the methods and habits by which orchids manage to insure the right cross-pollination, it becomes clear why it is difficult to describe them without resorting to such anthropomorphic terms as "manage," "ingenious," and "devious."

Logic would seem to indicate that the simplest way to attain the goal of fertilization, in view of the fact that the pollinia are located close to the stigma in the bisexual orchid flower, would be a mechanism for self-pollination. The fact is that, in the 3 percent noted above of self-pollinating, or cleistogamous, orchids, the

flowers do not open at all. But even in the normally outcrossing types, self-pollination may become an emergency solution if pollinating insects fail to visit the plant; if all else fails, the orchid can also propagate by producing offshoots—a means mentioned earlier as vegetative—which many do as a matter of course anyway.

Nonetheless, the great majority of orchids generally depend upon cross-pollinization; and, naturally, the variety of pollinators and their habits and tastes determine the devices by which the orchids manage to attract them. A few species are fertilized by birds such as nectareaters and hummingbirds, but these are relatively isolated cases; the majority of orchid pollinators are insects.

Hummingbird pollinating a South American *Laelia.*

The orchid-visiting insects cover a wide range. The most common, most numerous of these insects are bees of various, mostly solitary species. Some, especially in the temperate zones, are bumblebees, the social insects closely related to the honeybees. In the tropics the orchid-pollinating bees are predominantly members of a group with solitary habits—meaning that they do not live in hives. Known as euglossid bees, these are handsome, often brilliantly metallic insects with long tongues—and an equally long sting, with which they manage to protect themselves very efficiently against most enemies. These bees, especially the species of the type genus *Euglossa,* are so clearly the most important of the tropical orchid pollinators that they have become known as "orchid bees."

But there are a great number of other insects that function as pollinators for various types of orchids, including butterflies, moths, wasps, flies, and even gnats and mosquitoes. Each of these has to be attracted in specialized ways that take into account not only its size and other anatomical features such as the length of the proboscis, but also its individual senses and predilections.

Swallowtail butterfly visiting an Epidendrum *species.*

Color and scent are of course the two main factors in attracting insects, because both their sense of smell and their color vision are acute, even though the extent and range of their color perception may vary considerably. Bees, for example, cannot see red, but are drawn to yellow, blue-green, and all blue and violet hues including mauve, lavender, and purple. Their vision deficiency at the red end of the spectrum is compensated for at the other end by their ability to perceive ultraviolet, which to us is invisible. Because many flowers reflect ultraviolet, bees visiting certain blossoms may be reacting to color combinations we cannot see.

Butterflies, on the other hand, can perceive red and are attracted especially by all red, pink, and orange hues. The same is true of birds, for which bright red is the most alluring color—undoubtedly the reason why the orchids regularly visited by hummingbirds have red flowers.

Scent is apparently more universally important to orchids than color is. Even brightly hued orchids usually have a distinct and often very strong fragrance. It is the long-distance advertising, so to speak, which manages to entice the insects from far away, until they are close enough so the coloring of the blossom can take over as the main display. But in many cases, the scent has to do the entire job of attracting the insect, either because the orchid blossom is inconspicuously colored or because it is rendered colorless through prevailing circumstances, as is the case with all orchids fertilized by night-flying insects. Since it would serve no purpose to have bright colors in the dark, such orchids usually have white or very light-colored blossoms that emit a very strong fragrance, especially during the night, that unfailingly lures the moths which pollinate them.

Probably the most spectacular and convincing examples of the prime importance of scent are the species of the unusual genus—unusual even for orchids—*Catasetum*. These are sometimes called "Darwin's orchids," because the habits of this probably most highly

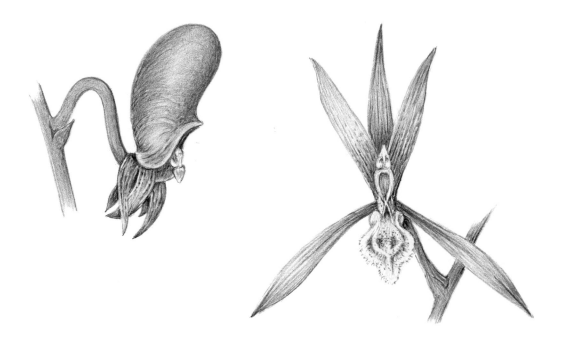

Extreme sexual dimorphism in a Catasetum *species: female flower, at left, and male flower, at right.*

organized of all orchid groups so captivated the English naturalist that he conducted especially painstaking studies of them, reporting the results in detail in his classic book.

The *Catasetum* orchids, which occur from Mexico to Brazil, are exceptional not only in that they are rarely bisexual, usually growing male and female flowers on separate plants quite far apart, but also in that the male flowers show a tremendous variety in shape and coloring, while the female flowers of the various species look very much alike. This, of course, makes identification difficult; and the *Catasetum* is one of the genera whose sex differences have in the past resulted in erroneous classification.

The most unusual feature, however, is the mechanism of pollination evolved by these orchids. The flowers of some of the most common species are an inconspicuous greenish-white or -yellow hue, not especially attractive to insects. Yet the bees that pollinate *Catasetum*—males of euglossid species—are found in great numbers at these flowers especially in the early morning hours, when the orchids emit a strong odor of anise and ripe fruit. How irresistible this scent is to the bees was reported by an observer from Costa Rica who collected a *Catasetum* orchid one morning. The usually shy bees followed him unhesitatingly into the house and into the room to which he took the flower. When he put it away in a drawer in order to find out what the bees would do, he was astonished to see them, in a frenzy of eagerness, attempting to get into the drawer through the slits between the wood.

As the sun rises higher during the day, the *Catasetum*'s fragrance becomes less pronounced and finally fades altogether, and the visits of the bees stop as though by magic. This trait of emitting their scent only at certain hours or for limited periods is typical of many other orchids. Probably the most outrageously individualistic are the plants of those species that emit different scents in different locations!

The foul odors characteristic of certain orchids are probably designed to attract filth-loving flies and similar insects as pollinators for their usually inconspicuous and dull-colored flowers. Certain groups, for example the genus *Bulbophyllum*, have a preponderance of members with such ill-smelling, small, and homely blossoms.

The great majority of orchids, however, are distinguished by either beautiful colors or a pleasant fragrance, or both, with which to entice successfully the insects each species needs to achieve fertilization. Many orchids are highly specialized, geared to attract only a single type of bee, or—as in the *Catasetum* —only the male sex of that particular species of bee.

Once the insect has arrived at the orchid flower, the flower is well prepared to insure that the visit is not in vain. To make certain that pollination will result, most orchids set a richly appointed table, tucked away in the interior of the flower, tempting the visitor with food that may range from the simple nectar

A Bulbophyllum *species that has small, ill-smelling flowers.*

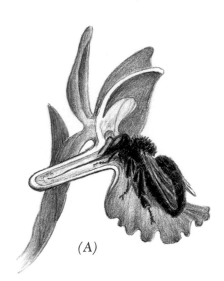

(A)

(B)

(C)

Pollination of an orchid, with a portion of the flower shown in cross-section: (A) Pushing its head into the nectary entrance, the bee touches the pollinia; (B) it withdraws from the flower, carrying the pollinia on its body; (C) when the bee visits the next orchid, the pollinia are in the right position for adherence to the stigma.

found also in many other blossoms to a variety of delicious tidbits with high nutritive value: sometimes a juicy, sugar-rich substance located in the spur; sometimes so-called food hairs, containing both sugar and protein; or special tissues that have a high content of various important nutrients. Bees masticate these often waxy or fatty substances until they become semiliquid and can be swallowed easily.

In many instances, the orchid is so engineered that the insect picks up its cargo of pollen even before it has located the food; as it enters the blossom, it inadvertently touches the clublike pollinia on the anther, and they adhere to its body with the help of the sticky substance secreted by the gland at the base of each pollinium. After the visitor has helped itself to the food, it leaves the flower without even realizing that it is decorated with the pollen packets. In the next orchid blossom, it has to pass the stigma on its way to the food source; in the meantime, the thin stems of the top-heavy pollinia have dried out enough to cause them to tip over into exactly the right position for easy adhesion to the stigma as the insect passes by, and fertilization is accomplished.

Among the many deviations and modifications of this basic arrangement developed by various orchids are some extremely intricate and sophisticated traps. Fine examples of these are found in the aforementioned *Catasetum* orchids, the males of which have two thin antennalike appendages known as wishbone antennae that protrude from the center of the flower into the path the bee has to take in order to get at the food it seeks. As soon as it crawls into the lip of a male *Catasetum*, it activates a trigger mechanism in the wishbone antennae. With great force the pollen packets are shot forth, execute a 180-degree turn in the air,

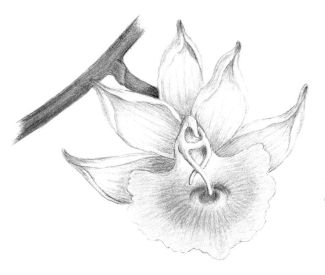

The wishbone antennae in a Catasetum *flower.*

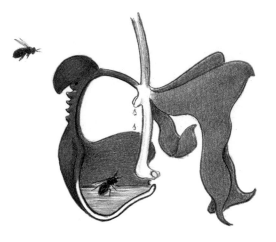

Diagram of a Bucket Orchid.

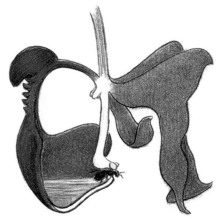

Color code

Lip: orange
Petals and Sepals: tan
Liquid: blue
Stigma: green
Column: white
Pollinia: yellow

involuntary bath, the bee is tempted by the rich food of the next Bucket Orchid, experiences the same adventure, and this time deposits the pollen on its way out.

Making the visiting insects slip and lose their footing seems to be a favorite trick of many orchids. *Gongora grossa,* for instance, is also so formed that its lip acts as the proverbial banana peel for the bee landing on it. As its feet slip, the bee falls on its back and slides down the curved column, picking up the pollinia on its abdomen as it passes the anther. On its next involuntary ride, it deposits the pollen on the stigma.

A variation of the banana-peel method is found in the Lady's Slipper, probably the most familiar and beautiful of all orchids of temperate zones. The lip of the Lady's Slipper is modified into the shoelike structure that has prompted its popular name, and is always brightly colored, usually in pinks and yellows. Most of these orchids have distinct and pleasing scents; the common yellow Lady's Slipper, for example, emits an apricot fragrance that proves very attractive to bees.

As soon as a bee, in response to the inviting fragrance, lands on the rounded, smooth lip surface, it slips and falls into the hollow "shoe" interior. Although it first tries to get out the way it came, the walls are so slippery that it is forced to seek another exit. It is then drawn toward the back of the flower, where light comes in through several transparent, windowlike areas. In seeking a way out there, it is doing exactly what it is supposed to do, for the exit is in fact near those windows. As the bee squeezes its way out, it passes the anther and picks up the pollinia, thus justifying the entire complex arrangement.

It must be said in all fairness that the food the insects receive for their troubles in these benevolent traps more than makes up for the inconvenience they have to endure. The Lady's Slipper, for instance, offers its visiting bees the delicious food hairs, rich in protein and sugar and well worth a little extra effort.

Other orchids are less forceful in their means of achieving the desired results. There is, for instance, the genus *Serapias*, whose members are generally distinguished by their hood- or helmet-shaped flowers, which make comfortable and convenient bedrooms for insects. The overnight guests cannot leave without paying for their rooms, of course: on the way out in the morning, they take along the pollinia and deposit them during their next visit to a *Serapias* orchid.

One genus of orchid that provides neither food nor room service practices perhaps the most surprising, and surely the most devious, of all means of attracting pollinators—the genus *Ophrys*, whose various species occur mostly in the warmer latitudes of the temperate zones. Many of the species are distinguished by a

Southern European Ophrys *species with visiting bees.*

resemblance to certain insects, usually bees. Because these orchids have no food—not even nectar—to offer to their visitors, some naturalists thought for a long time that the male bees regularly attending these flowers—and fertilizing them during vain attempts to mate with their insectlike lip—did in fact mistake the appearance of the labellum for a female bee.

Recent research, however, has yielded results that throw an entirely different light on this odd performance. Given the particular structure of the insect eye, many entomologists had always doubted that the bees were capable of recognizing the resemblance of the lip to the female bee, as the likeness is too farfetched in many cases. When the researchers discovered that each *Ophrys* emits the specific sexual odor of the female of the pollinating species, the Case of the Frustrated Male was solved, the fantastic fact established—that these orchids have evolved the most erotic lure imaginable to attract their involuntary helpers. And once the bee has landed, the hairy or velvety surface of the lip furthers the illusion. Stimulated by both odor and texture, the male tries to mate with the flower, and pollination is achieved through pseudocopulation.

Blossoms of three different Ophrys *species.*

In all of plantdom, it would be difficult to find anything that can match the sophistication—the sheer sensual trickery—of this device!

Unfortunately, and precisely because of their sophisticated schemes for fertilization, the future of certain orchids appears to be rather doubtful. Ecologists worry about the highly specialized types that have to depend on a single species of insect for pollination. Should these insects disappear, the orchids would be doomed along with them. The danger of that happening to certain types of orchids seems imminent in at least some parts of Central America, where the ecology of large areas is being significantly altered by the remorseless onslaught of man. One interesting as well as alarming report from Costa Rica illustrates the sensitivity of the ecological balance and the hazards any alteration of certain ecosystems immediately creates for a variety of organisms. Zoologist Daniel H. Janzen describes in a recent issue of *Natural History* magazine how the bulldozing of large areas of rain forest to create pasture for cattle has all but doomed a variety of flowering plants by eliminating the bees that pollinate them. Among these bees are the euglossid species that fertilize a number of local orchids including the famous *Catasetum*. It must be expected on the basis of these developments that sooner or later, when the old plants have all died, there will be no new orchids to replace them, and these species will become extinct. This unhappy conclusion pinpoints the urgency of proceeding with caution, common sense, and a willingness to consider all the ecological factors in changing any existing environment, lest we lose forever—and at an ever-increasing rate—too many of the unique and wonderful forms of life that today still enrich our planet.

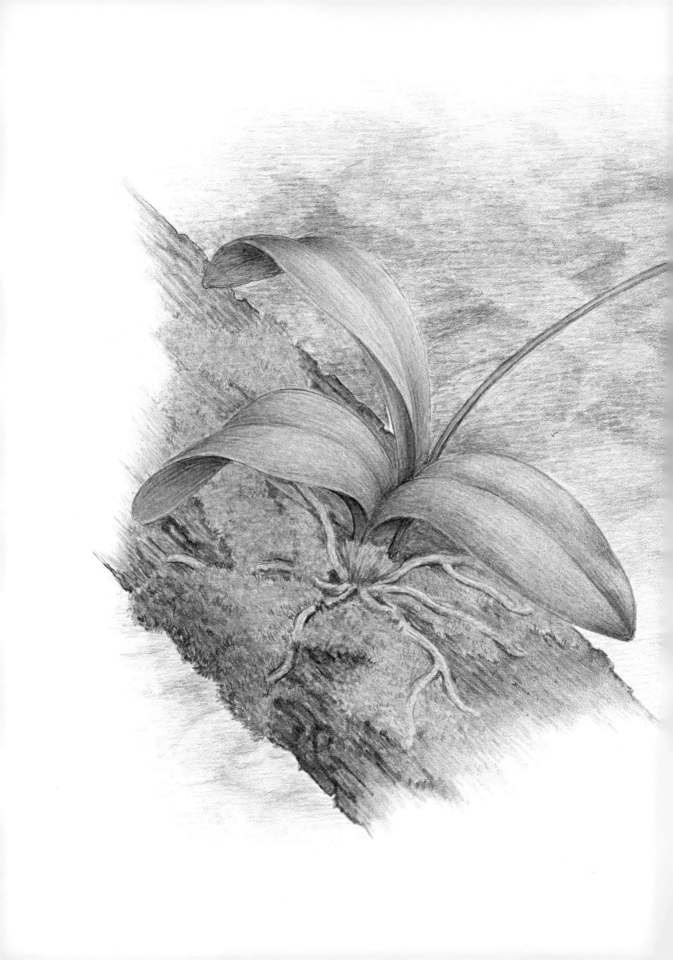

Phalaenopsis amabilis, *a lovely tropical orchid found in the Himalayas.*

A Showcase of Tropical Orchids

CONSIDERING THE PRODIGAL VARIETY and beauty of the tropical orchids, it is not surprising that different connoisseurs of these fabulous flowers have different favorites. Some enthusiasts may claim first place for the splendid *Cattleya;* others for the exquisite *Phalaenopsis,* the lovely *Dendrobium,* or the extravagant *Gongora.* The list could be continued to include many of the more than seven hundred genera that make up the orchid family. Each of the tropical groups has at least several dozen species; *Odontoglossum* counts no less than three hundred, and *Dendrobium* tops the list with some fifteen hundred.

An entire book with eye-filling pictures could be devoted to any one of the tropical genera, but within the confines of a single chapter, it is impossible to encompass more than some general information about these orchids, their life styles, and their ecology; and more detailed descriptions of a selection of especially interesting, unusual, or beautiful members of the various groups.

The great majority of tropical orchids are epiphytic, growing on trees both living and dead. Because orchids are not parasitic, the tree serves only as an anchoring place. There are also many terrestrial orchids in the tropics, and still others are capable of adapting to either life style. Although many flourish in the warm, humid atmosphere of the junglelike cloud and rain forests, others need the cool air at high altitudes of mountain ranges such as the Himalayas and the Andes to develop properly. And even though the popular image of the tropical orchid as an exotic-looking, strikingly colored flower with a sweet and heavy fragrance holds true for a great many kinds, there are also numerous others with small, inconspicuous, dull-colored, and often evil-smelling blossoms.

In adopting the epiphytic way of life, the majority of tropical orchids—like many other tropical epiphytes—assured themselves a place in the light that cannot be found in the permanent green twilight which prevails on the floor of the dense tropical forests. The need for light forced them up into the trees, where they developed a life style usually reserved either for lower plant forms such as mosses or lichens, or for parasites that take nourishment from their hosts, which no orchid does. Only the species of the warm latitudes, where temperatures never drop far enough to endanger the unprotected root system, were able to evolve as epiphytes.

Despite the great advantages of mild temperatures throughout the entire year, the epiphytes have their own considerable problems of survival. Because there is no nourishing soil from which their roots can draw the various mineral salts necessary for normal plant development, they have to depend upon other ways of getting these vital nutrients. A special mechanism found among plants living in regions with a high atmospheric humidity aids the epiphytes in solving this particular problem. To see how the mechanism works, one has to understand that one of the most vital functions of a plant—a tree, for instance—is the continuous cycling of water that is taken up by the roots and distributed to every part of the plant's system, until finally the excess moisture is evaporated through the leaves. Should this cycle be arrested or even disrupted for any length of time, the plant would die.

Such disruption is an ever-present danger in areas where a very high humidity makes it all but impossible for plants to evaporate the excess water in their systems. To maintain the vital cycle, plants in those regions have developed means of compensating for the lack of normal evaporation: special cells in the leaves called hydathodes—literally, waterways—which have the ability to excrete water and so keep the cycle intact. This water, which is rich in mineral salts, forms little droplets on the leaves of such tropical plants and is commonly mistaken for dew. The next rain—or even a heavy accumulation of the droplets themselves—washes this mineral-rich water down from the higher branches of the trees and onto the epiphytic plants that grow below. Such plants are adapted to absorb greedily the vital chemicals from the water.

Another problem facing the epiphytic orchids is that of preventing dehydration, which may sound peculiar in view of the frequency of rains in those regions and the high humidity of the atmosphere. However, it must be remembered that dry periods are common in most tropical zones, and also that epiphytic orchids are located in places where the rain water runs straight off and has no chance to collect. One reason why orchids prefer trees with rough bark is that small quantities of water, as well as moldering leaves, are trapped in the crevices formed by the bark. That water, however, is not sufficient; the epiphytic species have to supplement it by a water storage system which in many ways is similar to that employed by cactuses and other plants of arid regions.

A most important role in this water conservation falls to the pseudobulbs typical of the epiphytic, but also of some terrestrial and semiterrestrial, tropical orchids. The pseudobulbs—the thickened stems mentioned earlier—come in a variety of sizes and shapes and can store a considerable amount of water against dry spells. Some of these growths are tall and thin, others squat and roundish. The smallest measure no more than half an inch, whereas the largest, which consist of numerous segments, may grow to a height of more than twenty feet. There are even some pseudobulbs that contain cavities used as nests by certain ants without harming the orchid.

The water-conserving function of the pseudobulbs is augmented by the leaves and stems of many orchids, for they are thick and fleshy, with a tough, leathery texture that helps protect against dehydration. Also aiding in the utilization of all available resources are the air roots of many epiphytes; these have a highly specialized mechanism for condensing and absorbing moisture directly from the atmosphere. They can "breathe," too, meaning that they are capable of assimilating carbon dioxide from the air and utilizing it for the orchid's household.

Because of the popularity of the orchids belonging to the epiphytic genus *Cattleya,* so often called queen of them all, it is perhaps best to start off the parade of tropical species with these handsome, usually big and showy orchids from the American tropics. Cattleyas are found over a wide range extending all the way from Mexico to Argentina and Peru. Brazil has an especially large share of the sixty-five species that make up this genus, but most other South and Central American countries have at least a few indigenous species.

According to the number of leaves that rise from the typically prominent pseudobulbs, botanists distinguish two different groups of cattleyas: the unifoliate and the bifoliate species. In the unifoliate type, a single leaf sheathes the stem; the bifoliates have of course two leaves. With few exceptions, the usually short flower spike rises from the top of the pseudobulb that also bears the leaf or leaves.

Depending on the species, each flower stalk may have just a single blossom, or it may bear a cluster of up to twenty or even thirty flowers. It would be natural to assume that such clusters are typical of only those species whose individual blossoms are small, but that does not hold true for the *Cattleya* species. As a matter of fact, the largest of them all, appropriately named *C. gigas*, or

A typical unifoliate cattleya, the pale-colored C. gaskelliana.

A *typical bifoliate cattleya, the pretty* C. skinneri.

giant, which may attain a flower size of between eight and eleven inches across, sometimes has clusters bearing more than half a dozen of these huge flowers. Similarly, the beautiful bifoliate *C. violacea* with its five-inch blossoms usually displays at least six of these magnificent flowers on a single stalk.

The Cattleya orchids run strongly to pink, lavender, and white hues. The lip is usually much darker, and frequently of an entirely different color, so that it becomes very conspicuous. Its shape is also very distinctive, for the side lobes usually curve over the column to form a trumpetlike tube, and the margins of the frontal lobe are often ruffled. Although *Cattleya* shares these features with a number of other orchids, no other group has so many species distinguished by the large, trumpet-shaped labellum.

Cattleya forbesii.

Color variation among the individual species is another characteristic of the *Cattleya* genus. The same orchid may occur with white, pink, or amethyst-purple flowers. Yellow hues are less frequently found among the cattleyas, but a very beautiful and very rare pale-yellow species comes from the Peruvian Andes. The large four- to six-inch flowers of *C. rex* may grow in clusters of up to half a dozen; the labellum is deeply ruffled, and delicately marked with purple and gold.

Among the bifoliate cattleyas, a great number have mottled or spotted flowers; the lip of these orchids may differ markedly in shape, thus giving them a somewhat untypical appearance. A good example is *C. guttata*, with yellowish, purple-spotted sepals and petals and a white-and-red lip. On the other hand, the bifoliate *C. bowringiana* is a typical representative of this genus. A flower cluster of this deep pink Central American species with up to twenty three-inch blossoms on a single stalk is a sight to behold.

Cattleya guttata.

Closely related to the *Cattleya* orchids are those of the genus *Laelia*, with about the same number of species. They usually have narrower petals, and a smaller and less showy lip. A species from Guatemala with graceful, arching flower spikes bearing several pale-amethyst blossoms is locally called "Flor de Jesus."

Variations that are extraordinary even for orchids, both in plant form and in the size and shape of flowers, are found among

Guatemala's Flor de Jesus,
Laelia rubescens.

The well-known Cockleshell Orchid.

the more than a thousand species that make up the genus *Epidendrum*. Some of these orchids occur in the southern parts of the United States, but the majority are tropical, ranging from Mexico to Argentina. Among them are odd-looking flowers with narrow sepals and a conspicuous, upright lip such as *E. cochleatum*, known in England as the Cockleshell Orchid, and famed for being the first epiphytic orchid to bloom there in 1787. Cockleshell Orchids range from Florida to Brazil.

Other *Epidendrum* species may look like miniature *Cattleya* blooms, and still others, such as *E. ciliare,* have spidery flowers with very narrow, long sepals and petals.

A predilection for high elevations is characteristic of most members of the large genus *Odontoglossum,* which otherwise are

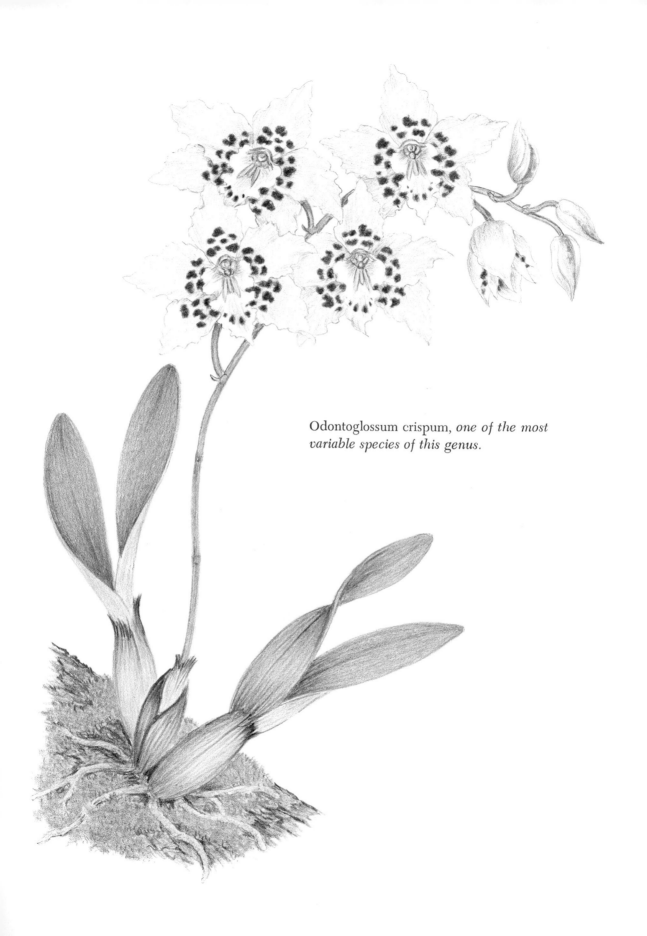

Odontoglossum crispum, *one of the most variable species of this genus.*

frequently distinguished by the mottled or spotted patterns of their flowers. The magnificent *O. grande,* known as the Tiger Orchid, which grows in Guatemala, has flowers up to six inches across, colored in rich hues of gold, brick, and brown. The most unusual species in the group, however, is *O. crispum,* in which the flowers of individual plants may vary so considerably in shape, color, and pattern that they appear to be separate species.

A great number of often very pretty and graceful orchids are gathered in the genus *Oncidium,* most of whose members are

The Tiger Orchid.

The Butterfly Orchid of the genus Oncidium.

found in South America. The majority of these usually rather small-flowered orchids are yellow, but white, pink, and brown hues also occur. The blossoms of some kinds are arranged on long arching spikes in groups reminiscent of ballet dancers, hence their popular name Dancing Ladies. The most famous of all the oncidiums, and one of the largest as well as the most spectacular, is the Butterfly Orchid, *O. papilio*. This was the fantastic-looking flower that first aroused world-wide interest in orchids more than a century ago. The large blossoms with their warm gold-and-brown hues are produced singly in succession on long, upright flower stalks.

Moving away from the American tropics, we find a number of interesting, unusual, and beautiful orchid groups in Asia and Africa. The most primitive of those are the tropical relatives of the well-known Lady's Slippers of the genus *Paphiopedilum*, many of which are found in the Himalayas, in Thailand, Burma, and other parts of southeast Asia. Most of these species have peculiar, large, waxy flowers that look almost artificial and are usually not distinguished by bright colors, often displaying greenish, brownish, and dull-purple shades. These species are mostly terrestrial, although some may grow on rocks; the majority have only a single flower on each stalk.

Australia, the home of so many strange and unique types of fauna and flora, runs true to form with many of its orchids, harboring numerous bizarre-looking species. Apart from such oddities as the Trapdoor Orchid and *Rhizanthella*, the subterranean orchid mentioned earlier—and to be discussed in a later chapter—we find other eccentric kinds, including the peculiar Spider Orchid, *Caladenia patersonii*, with its curled, bearded lip and long, narrow, tapering sepals and petals.

The showiest and largest of the Australian orchids are mostly members of the huge genus *Dendrobium*, whose members are found throughout the Asian tropics. All of them are epiphytic; flowers are produced singly or in pairs in some species; others grow in dense clusters of up to twenty individual blossoms. One of the best-known Australian species is *D. phalaenopsis*, whose color may vary from deep pink to pure white, with numerous hues and color combinations in between. The species is often used for hybridization.

Other handsome *Dendrobium* species include the lavender-colored *D. superbiens*, with strongly scented, four-inch flowers,

Paphiopedilum insigne, *an Asiatic Lady's Slipper, native to Assam, under cultivation since 1820.*

pretty *D. nobile,* and the pure-white *D. formosum,* with its large, long-lasting flowers. An impressive gold-colored species from the Himalayas is *D. fimbriatum,* with an almost round, fringed lip; the three-inch flowers grow at the upper part of the stem in drooping clusters of about half a dozen blossoms.

Among the connoisseurs' candidates for the "most beautiful" title are certain very special species of the two following genera.

Dendrobium fimbriatum, *found at high altitudes in the Himalayas.*

Coelogyne cristata *of the Himalayas is widely cultivated.*

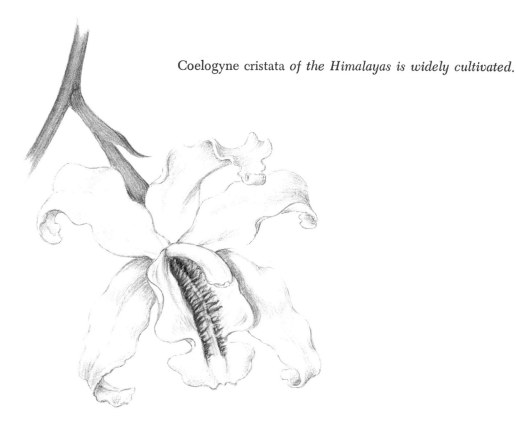

Coelogyne is the larger of the two groups with some hundred and twenty species, many from the cool mountain regions of the Himalayas. Its more spectacular members include *C. pandurata*, with a striking pale-green flower whose lip is predominantly black. It is called the Green Orchid, and also the Black Orchid —obviously an exaggeration, as the lip is only a small part of the flower.

Another Himalayan member of the group is *C. cristata*, thought to be one of the most beautiful orchids ever cultivated. The lip of its pure-white, four-inch flower is decorated with golden-colored, fringed ridges.

Phalaenopsis also has a number of exquisite species that range from the Philippines and New Guinea to India and Formosa. Commonly known as Moth Orchids because their shape suggests to some a moth with outspread wings, the flowers of these species are not especially large, but their elegant form and often delicate coloring place them among the most beautiful of all orchids. The spikes rarely have only one or two flowers; in the majority, the graceful arching or drooping stem bears from six to twenty, usually averaging two or three inches across. *P. amabilis*—often called the Butterfly Plant—is one of the largest and showiest of these orchids; its four-inch flowers are pure white with odd-shaped gold-stained lips, and the spike may bear up to twenty individual blossoms. The pale pink or mauve flowers of *P. schilleriana* and those of lovely *P. stuartiana* are arranged in similar sprays.

Another important and frequently cultivated Asiatic group is the genus *Vanda,* which ranges from China to northern Australia. It includes *V. coerulea,* a beautiful species from the Himalayas and Burma, and one of the relatively few blue orchids. The plant may grow to a height of about three feet and usually has about half a dozen flowers on each spike. To orchid growers, handsome *V. sanderiana* is one of the most important species of this genus because it can be used extensively for hybridization. Its large flowers, which may measure up to five inches across, are divided into a pink upper half and a yellowish, red-veined lower portion. The lip of this and many other *Vanda* species is small; others, such as the attractive, semiclimbing *V. teres,* have rather large and brightly colored labella.

The peculiar shape of the lip with its tonguelike appendage in the back accounts for the genus name of *Trichoglottis,* which is otherwise noteworthy because it includes another one of the so-called black orchids—*T. philippinensis,* which is actually a very dark maroon-purple.

Another tropical Asiatic group used extensively for cultivation and hybridization is *Cymbidium,* which has only about seventy species, but several thousand horticultural hybrids. Although these orchids originally come from China, Burma, and

The Himalayan Vanda coerulea, *one of the rare blue orchids.*

Cymbidium hookerianum, *an Asiatic species of an extensively hybridized genus.*

Japan, many of their large-flowered hybrids are today grown outdoors in flowers beds in such places as California. A handsome species is *C. hookerianum,* with large green flowers that have a yellow, purple-spotted lip.

So far, Africa has not been represented at all among the various species. This is because Africa runs a poor third in both numbers and variety; the great majority of tropical orchids are found in the Americas and in Asia. Two important African groups are *Disa* and *Angraecum,* each with some two hundred different species. The genus *Disa* is distinguished not only by the fact that it includes one of the few bright-blue orchids, but also by the peculiar modification of its petals, which are frequently small and inconspicuous, including the lip—in sharp contrast to the great majority of all other orchids. Another distinguishing characteristic is the middle sepal, which is often hooded as well as spurred. Colors are generally bright; in addition to the blue *D. graminifolia*, there are such vividly colored species as *D. uniflora* from South Africa, with flowers that combine scarlet with bright pink or orange.

Angraecum, on the other hand, has very few colorful varieties; the flowers of nearly all these African and Madagascan species are white, ivory-colored, or greenish. Many have a distinctive starlike shape; the Star-of-Bethlehem Orchid illustrated in the first chapter is typical of this group. The white, fragrant flowers of most *Angraecum* orchids with their medium-to-long spurs indicate that these species are pollinated by various night-flying moths.

Disa graminifolia, *a blue orchid found in Africa.*

Orchids of the
Temperate Zones

To WHAT EXTENT ORCHIDS are basically offspring of the warmer, tropical latitudes of our planet becomes clear when we compare the number of species found in the temperate regions with those in any given tropical zones. Whereas all of Europe, for instance, can boast of only about sixty different kinds, a single South American country such as Brazil counts its orchid species in the hundreds.

In North America, the lines are not as clearly drawn; geographically, Central America, which also harbors hundreds of orchid species, is part of the North American continent. But if Central America is considered separately for purposes of orchid grouping, Canada and the United States still have more than twice the species found in Europe. This can be explained partly by the fact that some subtropical orchids, including certain epiphytic kinds, range into such southern parts of the United States as Florida and southern California. Thus the leafless vanilla, *V. barbellata,* grows in hammock soil in southern Florida, as do several species of *Epidendrum* including the famous Cockleshell Orchid. Southern California hosts Mexican orchids such as the hummingbird-pollinated *Comparettia,* and one or two *Cattleya* species.

In the rest of the United States and Canada, however, we find only the usually small-flowered, terrestrial orchids typical of all temperate zones. Many of these species belong to genera also well represented in Europe and temperate Asia, although some are restricted to the Western Hemisphere, just as there are others that are found only in Eurasia.

In addition to having relatively few indigenous kinds, the temperate zones harbor some orchids that have become so rare that nature lovers consider themselves fortunate when they discover one of these plants in bloom. Nature groups in some countries organize special hikes designed to locate orchids for the purpose of keeping track of the number occurring in a given region. Most orchids are rigorously protected in many parts of Europe; violators risk stiff fines if caught picking, collecting, or transplanting them in defiance of the "nature protection" law designed to preserve the indigenous flora and fauna. This law applies even to the more common species—which are very special wild flowers, nevertheless, that must not be endangered.

As mentioned earlier, only terrestrial orchids whose root systems are well protected against the winter cold can live in the cooler latitudes. From their tuberous roots, new stems with leaves grow every year in the spring, and usually, but not always, the new growth will bear flowers later in the season.

The typical orchid of temperate zones rarely exceeds thirty inches in height; most are considerably shorter, averaging between ten and fifteen inches. The stem is usually straight, is relatively thick and fleshy, and ends in a terminal spike that bears the flowers, which in the majority of species number more than one or two and are often arranged either spirally or in a pyramid-like cluster. Blossoms are rarely more than an inch across; most are considerably smaller.

The leaves, which may be broad or narrow and grasslike, often

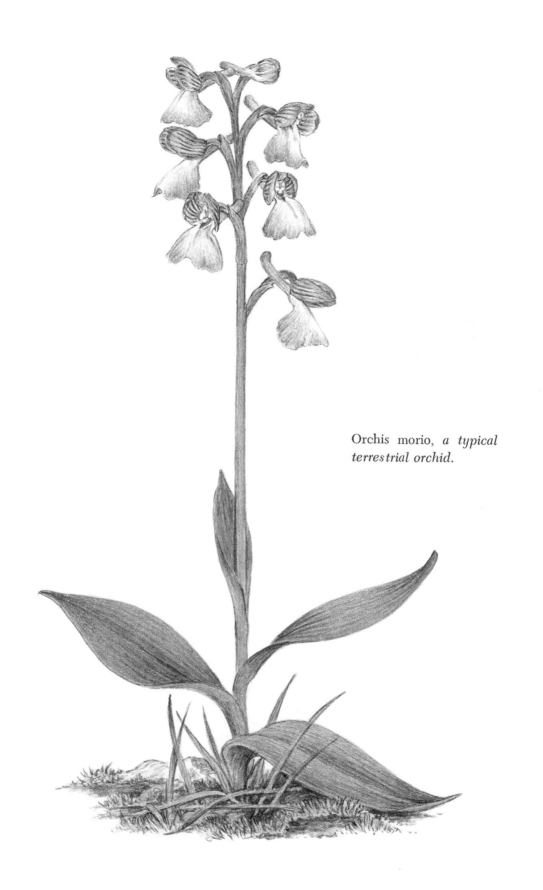

Orchis morio, *a typical terrestrial orchid.*

Orchis palustris, *the European Swamp Orchid.*

grow only at the plant base, where they usually sheathe the stem; in many species, however, smaller leaves develop higher up on the stalk and even between the flowers of the cluster. The colors vary considerably, although the most common hue seems to be some shade of pink, ranging from pale to purplish. Many are white, or greenish-white, and yellow; deep golden, orange, and bright scarlet flowers occur less often.

A number of the terrestrial orchids are rather narrowly confined to a particular environment. Some, for example, can grow only in very wet, swampy areas. A rare and handsome European species, the Swamp Orchid, *Orchis palustris,* is limited to bogs and wet moors. Another much more common European moisture-loving orchid is *Dactylorhiza majalis,* which frequently grows near springs.

At the opposite end are the mountain orchids; those of the genus *Nigritella* prefer sunny slopes at altitudes varying from

Nigritella nigra, *a European mountain orchid.*

3000 to 5000 feet and occur at such elevations in the Alps, the Pyrenees, and the Apennines. Not very orchidlike in appearance, as their popular German name, *Kohlröschen,* "little cabbage rose," indicates, they have narrow leaves, a sturdy stem, and a small, tightly bunched cluster of flowers on a terminal spike. The color may vary from a black-stained bright red to orange-yellow; the flowers emit a strong, delicious vanilla fragrance which bees find irresistible. Even more of a mountain climber is *Chamae-orchis alpina,* a dwarf species of the windswept rocky slopes of the Alps at altitudes between 5000 and 8000 feet, where it grows next to such other purely alpine flowers as the legendary edelweiss.

One of the most peculiar of specialized orchid life styles distinguishes the species that are saprophytes, organisms living on dead or decaying organic matter. These orchids have lost all capability for photosynthesis, the process of assimilating carbon dioxide from the air and forming carbohydrates in chlorophyll-containing tissues. Because they have no chlorophyll, or at least practically none, they have no green coloring either. Incapable of furnishing their own food in the manner of normal plants, they have become entirely dependent upon certain fungi which help them to get nutrients from dead organic matter such as decaying wood and leaves. Even the water supply is handled by the in-dispensable fungus partners, which makes it clear why orchids of this type are narrowly restricted to humus- and moisture-rich habitats.

Their lack of chlorophyll lends these orchids a peculiarly pale, "dead" appearance unlike that of the typical plant, which has given rise in the past to some sinister superstitions. Actually, there is nothing at all sinister about them; they are not poison-ous, and their flowers, though small, are frequently very pretty. The European *Neottia nidus-avis*—the Bird's Nest Orchid—whose pale ivory or sand-colored leaves sheathe an equally pale stem, has brownish flowers that emit a pleasant honeylike fragrance,

which attracts insects eager to find the nectar offered to them in
the cup-shaped posterior part of the flower's lip. Apart from its
peculiar color, the most unusual feature of this plant is its root
system—a tangled mass whose likeness to an untidy bird's nest
gave it its scientific and popular names.

*The Bird's Nest Orchid occurs widely
throughout Europe.*

The most distinctive feature of Corallorhiza *is its root system.*

Other saprophytes are found in various parts of the world. The genus *Corallorhiza*, with species both in Europe and in North America, is distinguished by rootstocks that resemble coral growths. The European member of this group may have some traces of chlorophyll in its pale, greenish-yellow leaves and stems, although the plants usually are almost colorless. A common North American species is *C. maculata*, with a range extending from Nova Scotia to the Pacific and the subtropical regions of Central America. It is much more brownish than the European species, with leafless, tan-colored stems and small brown flowers with a purple-spotted white lip.

Another leafless saprophyte is *Epipogium aphyllum* of Europe, a rare species that is locally known as the Glass Orchid. It is almost transparent in all its parts and looks so fragile that one expects it to break when touched. The leafless stems are pale yellowish or tan, the relatively large blossoms white and translucent like alabaster. They have a pleasant banana fragrance and a spur that contains the nectar for the pollinating insects.

The Glass Orchid.

The flowers of Spiranthes aestivalis *face in every direction.*

Despite the considerable number of such specialized kinds, the majority of orchids occurring in the cooler latitudes have shown a remarkable talent for adapting to a variety of habitats. Some do equally well in low-lying areas and at altitudes up to several thousand feet; others may grow in sunny, dry, open locations in one part of the world and in wet meadows and even bogs in another. Such adaptability has permitted certain species to have a tremendous range. Orchids of the genus *Spiranthes,* for instance, may be found from the Arctic regions all the way to parts bordering on the Antarctic. A common North American member of this world-wide group is S. *cernua,* popularly known as Nodding Ladies' Tresses, which ranges from Nova Scotia to Florida and the Southwest. It has long, slender leaves and tiny white flowers growing on a terminal spike in numbers usually exceeding a dozen.

Even the generally adaptable orchids of temperate zones, however, have an Achilles heel that is endangering many of them today. This weakness is their sensitivity to man-made changes in soil composition that affect the funguses with which orchids live in a symbiotic relationship. Artificial alterations such as those caused by chemical fertilizers, or drainage of low-lying areas, kill off the fungi and thereby doom most of the orchids. This was noticed frequently in Europe, where orchids disappeared abruptly after meadows had been treated with chemical fertilizers.

Best known among those orchids that have adapted to a variety of habitats in different parts of the world are the species of *Cypripedium,* the Lady's Slippers. The largest, showiest, and probably most loved of all the orchids of temperate zones, they also oddly enough are the most primitive—that is, this and related genera are considered the least advanced members of a highly advanced family.

A flower of the European Lady's Slipper.

Three Cypripedium *species: (from left to right) Pink Lady's Slipper; Moccasin Flower; Yellow Lady's Slipper.*

A reliable clue to whether a species of plant or animal is well known to the general public can be found in its popular or common name as distinguished from its scientific Latin name. Whenever a species has only the latter, the chances are that the average person is not familiar with it. On the other hand, if the species has not just one but several popular names, and possibly different names or modifications in different countries, that species is undoubtedly cosmopolitan as well as widely known and easily recognized. Such is the case with the Lady's Slipper orchids of the genus *Cypripedium*. Several species occur in North America, and while only one is found in Europe and Eurasia, that one is known in many languages.

The popular variations of "Lady's Slipper" in different languages all refer in some way to the shoelike shape of the lip. The English term is an almost exact translation of the German *Frauenschuh,* and both are traceable to the sixteenth century, when the name first appeared in homage to Mary, Mother of Christ. "Slipper of Our Lady" was later contracted to the present form; the Russian *Mariin Bashnachock*—"Mary's Slipper"—still has the original wording. The French, with characteristic Gallic imagination, were inspired not by religion but by an entirely different train of thought when they named the orchid *Sabot de Vénus.* The botanists who chose the scientific name agreed with the French, for *Cypripedium*, derived from the Greek, means the same thing. In the United States, various species are frequently called Moccasin Flowers, although Lady's Slipper is still the most widely used name.

The single European representative of the group is *C. calceolus*, a handsome species usually about a foot tall, but occasionally reaching twice that height. The leaves are broad and bright green; besides those that sheathe the stem at the base, there are smaller ones growing at the point where the short and slightly curved flower stalks join the stem. The flowers are quite large, up to four inches across, and usually number only one or two at the most. Petals and sepals, with the exception of the bright yellow lip, are brown or maroon-colored, often shading into purple. The two lower sepals are fused to form a broad double-tipped leaf beneath the "shoe"; the two remaining petals are long, narrow, and spirally twisted. The broad uppermost sepal bends forward over the conspicuous lip.

Although the Lady's Slipper is not one of the rare European orchids, it no longer is as widespread or as common as in the past. One hundred and fifty years ago, the noted German naturalist, world traveler, and statesman Alexander von Humboldt reported finding entire meadows of Lady's Slippers in the Ural mountains of Russia. Since then, changes in the environment and too much collecting and transplanting have considerably reduced the numbers of these orchids in the Eurasian regions.

In North America, the genus *Cypripedium* is represented by close to a dozen different species, which include those of the formerly separate genus *Fissipes*. Best known among the North American species are the Yellow, Pink, and Showy Lady's Slippers. The first is a variety of the European kind; the last, under its other name of Moccasin Flower, is the state flower of Minnesota. Its white-and-pink blossoms are quite striking, especially in combination with the bright green of the leaves.

It is interesting to note that the American and European Lady's Slippers, although closely related, prefer different habitats: the American Yellow Lady's Slipper, for instance, which is only a variety of the European species, occurs in moist, humus-rich woods, whereas the European kind likes open woods and is often found on sunny hillsides with lime-rich soil. The Moccasin Flower is even more extreme in its preference for moisture, occurring typically in bogs or in wet, swampy meadows.

Much less common and less familiar, but similar to the Lady's Slippers in that it has a solitary, fairly large, and attractive flower, is the genus *Calypso*, with only a single species indigenous to Eurasia as well as to North America. The plant is distinguished by

Calypso bulbosa, *the sole representative of an entire genus.*

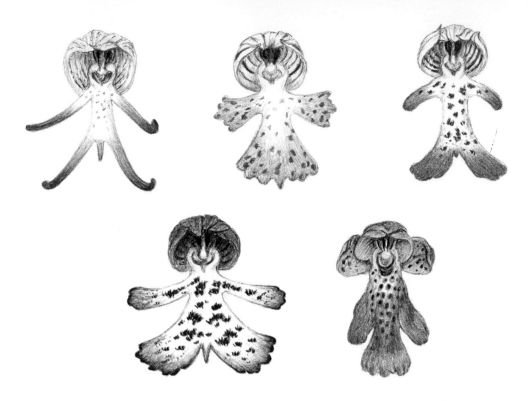

Single blossoms (enlarged about twice) of five European Orchis species, showing the helmetlike arrangement of petals and sepals above the column, and the deeply lobed lip. In the Monkey Orchid (upper row, left) the lobes form the arms and legs of the "monkey" for which the orchid was named.

an almost onion-shaped tuberous base, from which grows a single leaf that does not sheathe the flower stalk. The solitary flower has a partly hooded lip, above which the sepals and other petals form a crest.

The type genus *Orchis* is represented by numerous species in Europe, Asia, and North America. Although a few of them are very rare, others are quite common; the European *O. militaris*, so named because of the helmetlike appearance of its inch-long flowers, is widespread throughout many parts of Europe. A closely related but rare species is the Monkey Orchid, *O. simia*, whose oddly shaped lip resembles a tiny, grinning monkey.

The tallest of all orchids of the Eurasian regions is another member of this genus. *O. purpurea* may attain a height of almost three feet, although the average lies between fifteen and twenty inches. The terminal spike is five or six inches long and bears

European Butterfly Orchid of the genus Orchis.

dozens of usually purple-pink flowers with a four-lobed lip.

Distinguished by the great variability of color is a species of the genus *Dactylorhiza,* which is closely related to *Orchis. D. sambucina* often has bright-yellow flowers, but they also come in a number of other shades including orange and fiery red, and every so often a group of these orchids includes several color variations growing side by side.

Two color varieties of a Dactylorhiza *species.*

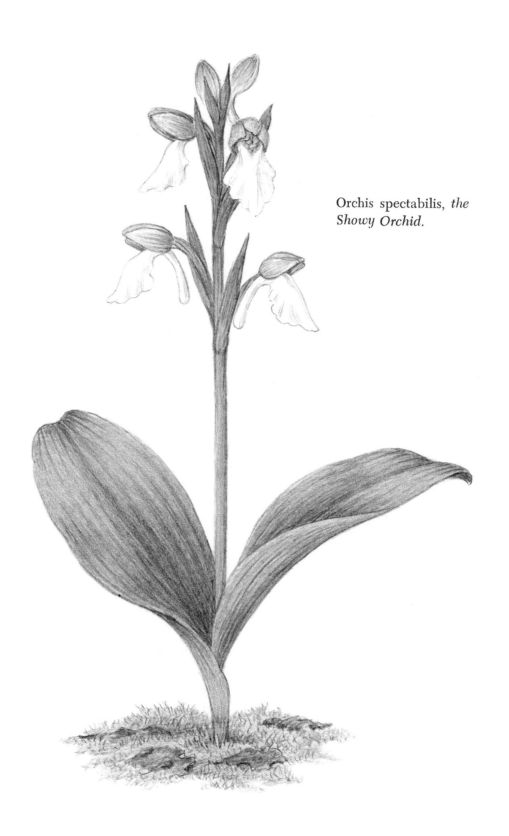

Orchis spectabilis, *the Showy Orchid.*

Several different *Orchis* species occur widely in the North American continent. One of the best-known, *O. spectabilis,* the Showy Orchid, is found in many parts of the eastern half of the United States and some southern areas of Canada. It grows to a height of about a foot, has two basal leaves that sheathe the stem, and several attractive pink-and-white flowers.

Comparatively few orchid genera are represented widely in both tropical and temperate regions: one of them is *Habenaria,* a large group of some five hundred species of world-wide distribution. All of them have flowers that are spurred at the base, indicating that their pollinators are insects with a long proboscis such as butterflies and moths. An elegant-looking and fragrant tropical species from Malaysia and China is *H. susannae* with large three- or four-inch flowers. Not so spectacular but also very attractive is the Yellow Fringed Orchid, *H. ciliaris,* one of the widest-ranging North American orchids. Its bright golden-yellow or orange flowers are about an inch across and distinguished by the fringed lip that is a hallmark of many *Habenaria* species.

One of the important orchid groups of temperate zones that is restricted to Eurasia and North Africa is the genus *Ophrys,* whose members have distinctive and relatively large flowers measuring an inch or so across. The flowers, usually numbering between two and six and loosely spaced along the stalk, are showy and colorful. As described in an earlier chapter, they often bear a resemblance to certain insects and use erotic lures

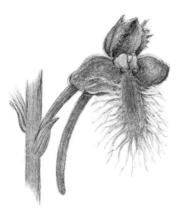

Single flower of the North American Yellow Fringed Orchid.

Ophrys *hybrids:* Ophrys bertolinii *(top row, center) hybridizes with* O. speculum *(left) and* O. tenthredinifera *(right) to produce the hybrids below.*

to attract male bees and wasps. Although this group numbers only about thirty species, there are a great many hybrids, because it is one of the orchid genera with a pronounced inclination toward natural hybridization. A study by botanists of these orchids on the island of Majorca, where they grow especially in the open pine woods, revealed five natural hybrids in addition to the seven species listed during this study. Color variations also occur frequently, as do different markings of the lip. Thus the same locality yielded two *O. tenthredinifera* plants, one with brown-and-pink, the other with bright-yellow flowers.

An attractive Ophrys *species.*

The temperate regions of eastern Asia and North America also have their indigenous species not found in other parts of the world. Pretty pink orchids with thin stems and grasslike leaves belonging to two different genera occur in various locations on the North American continent. One of these, the showy *Pogonia ophioglossoides,* popularly known as the Bearded Orchid, is common throughout the eastern half and ranges relatively far north. Its solitary two-inch flowers have a bearded, gold-stained lip. Similar in appearance, but members of a different group and much more widespread in distribution, the orchids of *Calopogon*

The Grass Orchid, Calopogon pulchellus, *survives on the wind-swept dunes of Sable Island off Nova Scotia.*

Pogonia ophioglossoides, *the Bearded Orchid of North America.*

Bletilla striata *of the temperate regions of the Far East.*

are found in wet, swampy meadows and bogs. They occur chiefly in the North American southeast and are common in Florida, but also occur in the Bahamas and Cuba.

A very hardy orchid of temperate regions of the Far East is *Bletilla striata.* Native to Japan, Taiwan, and China, it is frequently cultivated. And then there is the common Asian species that has become a weed in some southern parts of the United States. Introduced by accident, probably along with grass seed, it soon began to spread throughout the Gulf States, and today *Zeuxine strateumatica,* a short-stalked, multileaved orchid with small white blossoms, is firmly established in the southeast.

Even this partial review of the orchids of the temperate regions leaves no doubt that they are true members of a family known for its diversity. Despite severe restrictions imposed upon them by seasonal changes and other environmental hardships, they have managed to develop a fascinating variety of forms, colors, and life styles.

Mimics, Masks, and Other Oddities

ALTHOUGH BY NOW it has surely been demonstrated that the exceptional is the rule among orchids, that their uncommon features outnumber those they share, the very wealth of their oddities has made it impossible to include all of them in the foregoing chapters on the general plant structures and habits of orchids. Hence, this chapter has been reserved for a more detailed description of some of the most extraordinary, but sometimes isolated, phenomena in the orchid world.

One fact immediately apparent during even a cursory review of orchid names is the frequency with which they refer to animals and objects. There are the Monkey, Swan, and Flying-Bird Orchids; the Fly, Bee, Spider, Butterfly, and Moth Orchids; there is a Bucket Orchid, a Trapdoor Orchid, and a Punch-and-Judy Orchid. Human imagination, of course, inclines toward this finding of resemblances in nature; people see faces in rocks and clouds, masks and eyes in the wings of insects such as the Death's Head Moth, and similar, often far-fetched likenesses. Orchids especially encourage such flights of fancy by their often eccentric shapes, their intricate patterns and markings. So imitative do many of them seem that in at least one instance, that of the *Ophrys*

A Swan Orchid of the genus Cycnoches.

species, even naturalists tended to speak of these flowers as *mimicking* various insects. To see how such thinking came about, we only have to look at the Fly Orchid to realize that a case can be made out for a more than coincidental resemblance to an insect. Similarly, the Bee and Bumblebee Orchids, respectively, both have velvety-brown lips shaped somewhat like the body of a hymenopterous insect.

Nevertheless, we must be careful about applying the term "mimic" indiscriminately to plants because it is used correctly only for animals, especially insects, which in body shape, color, and design strongly resemble either such natural objects as leaves, flowers, and branches, or other well-armed creatures, and thereby gain a definite advantage—usually protection against enemies such as birds or lizards, or attraction of prey. Such mimicry occurs widely in the insect world, and frequently is so striking that the mimic disappears from view when it settles on the leaf or flower it resembles. Famous examples are the Leaf Butterfly of India, or the Walking Leaf insect from Malaysia.

The alleged mimicry by orchids of insects does not fall into the above-mentioned categories. As stated earlier, the rather vague resemblance of these *Ophrys* species to insects is all that is needed, because it is only a secondary aid in luring the pollinators

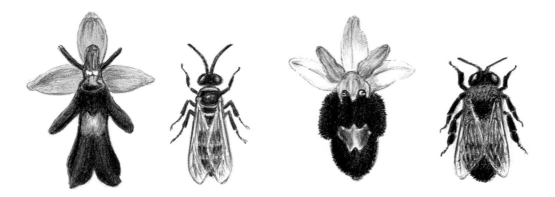

Ophrys *blossoms and the insects they supposedly mimic.*

The Scorpion Orchid.

in the shape and color of the orchid repeated in the various body parts of the mantis: the leg flanges widened to form petallike shapes; the green margin of the prothorax mimicking a portion of stem, and brown markings on the abdomen representing wilted leaf areas.

To strengthen the blossomlike appearance, the mantis assumes a stance in which the legs are spread wide like dangling petals, while the abdomen is raised high to look like a bud. Little wonder that even the keen and highly trained eyes of American naturalist Edward S. Ross, who encountered one of these mantises during his travels in Malaysia, at first completely overlooked the insect, mistaking it for a part of the orchid's flower cluster.

Although in the case of orchids true mimicry must thus be more or less discounted, it is still a fascinating exercise in imagination to look at some of these curious blossoms and appreciate their resemblance to a variety of objects and animals, sometimes vague, but frequently quite pronounced and unmistakable. Not all names likening orchids to objects are merely fanciful, of course; as we have already seen, the Bucket Orchid really has a bucket, the Lady's Slipper looks undeniably like a shoe, and the Trapdoor Orchid functions like a very sophisticated trap door. Others, of course, have at best a far-fetched resemblance to whatever object they are named for—it takes a great deal of imagination to see a swan, a spider, or a scorpion in the orchids that bear these names. On the other hand, there is the strange pure-white *Peristeria elata,* the national flower of the Republic of Panama, which is known as the Holy Ghost Orchid.

Holy Ghost Orchid. Note the column and lip at right that form the "dove."

Single flowers of the European Doll Orchid.

Also called the Dove Orchid, its combined column and lip form a shape strongly resembling a white dove with outspread wings and a fan-shaped tail.

Similarly, the European Doll Orchid—also known as the Mask Orchid—has a long, dangling, yellowish-brown man- or doll-shaped lip with arms and legs and a face shaded by a hood formed by the combined sepals and petals. As its scientific name *Aceras anthropophora* proves, even naturalists were impressed by the shape of the flower. For that matter, the fact that botanists often enjoy the game of "What does it look like?" is proved by a number of scientific names. The orchids of the genus *Ornithocephalus*—literally, bird's head—have anthers that resemble the head of a long-billed bird.

One orchid that fully justifies its name is the Hammer Orchid of western Australia. The curious lip of this odd-looking orchid not only is shaped like a hammer but acts like one. Hinged and touch-sensitive, it reacts with a hammerlike movement to any pressure applied to its tip. Although the reasons for this behavior pattern are not yet fully clear, it has been suggested that insects too large to act as proper pollinators are scared off by the movement caused by their weight on the lip.

Proceeding from oddities of shape and color of the flower to those of life style and growth pattern—in addition to those already discussed—the subterranean orchid mentioned earlier is unique among the saprophytes, with which it has been classified. This orchid was discovered only a few years ago when a farmer in Australia turned it up by accident while plowing his field. So unique is this one species that it has been classified as a separate genus, *Rhizanthella*: so far at least, no other orchids of this type have been found anywhere else in the world. Because

The weird flowers of the Hammer Orchid.

it is normally never exposed to light and of course has no chlorophyll, it must receive its nutrients from the soil. Its peculiar appearance starts with the pale, pinkish-white color of the entire plant; the tiny flowers, which measure only an eighth of an inch across, are arranged inside a blossomlike circle of leaves,

Rhizanthella, *the unique subterranean orchid of Australia.*

Flower and buds of Grammatophyllum speciosum.

making this perhaps the most atypical-looking of all orchids.

The most unusual of all the epiphytes is the giant of orchids, a member of the sparse genus *Grammatophyllum*. This huge orchid often grows on the stumps of large trees; under maximum conditions, its canelike pseudobulbs may attain a height of up to twenty-five feet, ending in leaves more than two feet long. A single one of these tree-sized orchids may bear a hundred flowers or more at a time, each of them five or six inches across and handsomely speckled in purple on a light-yellow background. No other orchid attains this size, although some of the other *Grammatophyllum* species grow to be quite large.

Another giant orchid is a species which, although it is slender and reedy instead of massive like *Grammatophyllum,* still reaches a height of fifteen feet. This plant is *Selenipedium chica,* a member of a tropical American genus of Lady's Slipper relatives. The flowers, which grow at the very top on a terminal spike, are relatively small, not more than a couple of inches across.

Then there are the dwarfs of orchiddom; many groups, including the Lady's Slippers, have their tiny members. Thus the tropical Asian Lady's Slippers of the genus *Paphiopedilum,* most of which average between fifteen and thirty inches high, include

Paphiopedilum bellatulum, *a dwarf Lady's Slipper.*

Oncidium glossomystax, *a miniature orchid of tropical America.*

a dwarf species whose smallness is determined less by the size of the flower than by the shortness of the stalk, which may measure no more than an inch or two.

Real miniatures are found among the various *Oncidium* species as well as among some other tropical American orchids. *Lepanthopsis vinacea,* for instance, is only between two and three inches tall, and its flowers measure only half an inch across. The members of the dwarf genus *Sophronitis* hardly ever grow more than three inches tall, although their flowers may be almost that size and therefore look top-heavy. The delightful little *S. coccinea,* for example, is quite literally as wide as it is high when in bloom, for it stands only three inches tall and its flower measures three inches across. Probably one of the tiniest of the dwarfs is *Maxillaria sophronitis* (not to be confused with the genus *Sophronitis*); it grows only two inches high and has miniature pseudobulbs and one-inch leaves and flowers.

Extreme modification of certain plant parts, such as the sepals and petals, is a prominent feature in a number of species of several different groups. There is, for instance, a South American relative of the Lady's Slippers that grows to a height of three feet. Incongruously, however, the petals of *Phragmipedium caudatum* also attain a length of three feet, and therefore often touch the ground even though the flower grows at the top of the stalk. A similar modification occurs in some other species; the tropical American *Brassia longissima,* for instance, has sepals

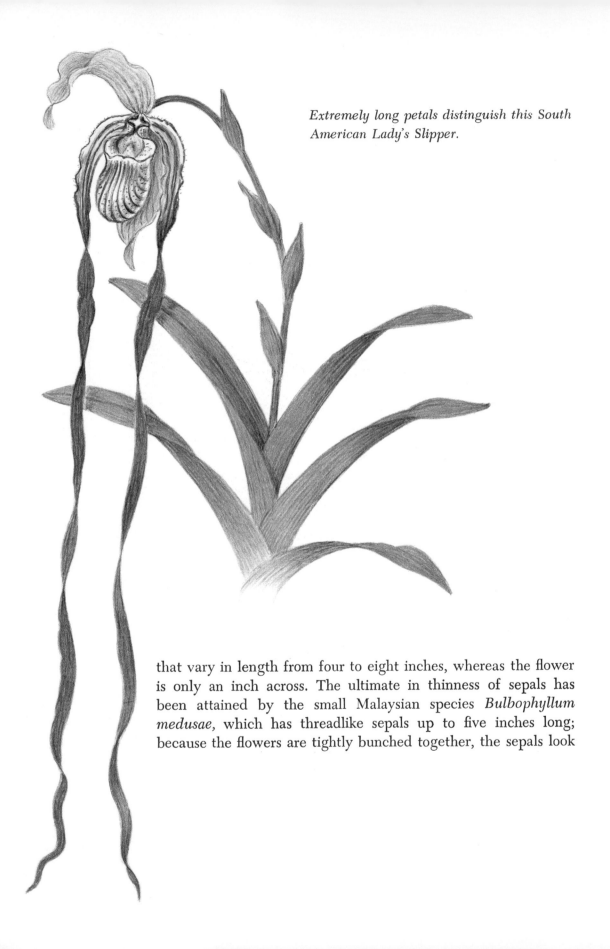

Extremely long petals distinguish this South American Lady's Slipper.

that vary in length from four to eight inches, whereas the flower is only an inch across. The ultimate in thinness of sepals has been attained by the small Malaysian species *Bulbophyllum medusae*, which has threadlike sepals up to five inches long; because the flowers are tightly bunched together, the sepals look very much like the tentacles of a jellyfish, hence the scientific name.

The various leaf shapes and their modifications already have been discussed to some extent; the strangest, unique even among

In this Brassia *species, the sepals are greatly elongated.*

the individualistic orchids, occurs in a single species of the large group *Dendrobium* and is native to Australia. Appropriately named the Cucumber Orchid—no flight of fancy in that name—*D. cucumerinum* has gherkinlike leaves about an inch long that grow directly from the rhizome without any stalk. Flowers are produced on a spike that develops at the base of the cucumber leaf.

Another very peculiar leaf shape is displayed by the Braided Orchids of the genus *Lockhartia*. The plant looks like a tightly woven braid, and the flowers grow from between the "strands" at the upper end of the plant.

Although fanlike growth patterns are frequently found among orchids, the rigid fan formed by the leaves and thickened leaf stems of tiny *Ornithocephalus bicornis* presents a unique appearance somewhat resembling the well-known feather fans displayed by peacocks during their courtship performance.

Possibly the oddest of the epiphytic types are those without any leaves at all. Although leafless terrestrial orchids have been

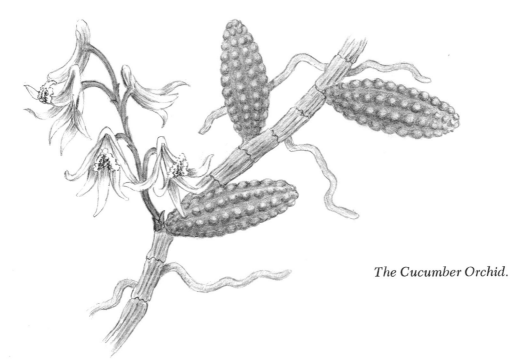

The Cucumber Orchid.

The Braided Orchid.

described in an earlier chapter, the leafless epiphytes are in a class by themselves. They have a unique root system, with individual branches sometimes a foot or more long. From these roots arise short flower stalks bearing showy ivory-white flowers that are spurred at the base—sure indications that they are pollinated

The leafless Ghost Orchid.

by night-flying moths. *Polyrrhiza lindenii,* which occurs in southern Florida and Cuba, has flowers that may be four or five inches long; it is often called the Ghost Orchid because of the peculiar shape of the flower, which suggests a ghostlike face.

Only a tiny percentage of known orchid species have been touched upon in this book. In the selection of a number of representative members of important groups, and the addition of especially notable species even from small and generally less well-known genera, an attempt has been made to offer a glimpse of the manifold wonders of orchid life.

A male Crestless Gardener Bowerbird of New Guinea, with a *Dendrobium* blossom in its beak. With the exception of man, this bird is the only animal that uses orchids for their beauty: it plucks the blossoms to decorate the entrance of the hutlike bower it builds of sticks and vines for its courtship display. The orchids are placed on a carpet of moss it has laid down at the bower entrance, and periodically it replaces the wilted blossoms with fresh ones to attract the female.

Geographical Ranges of Orchids

THE MAPS on the six following pages are designed to serve as graphic guides to the world-wide distribution of important groups in the orchid family. Whereas some of the largest and most familiar genera of each continent are depicted and named with labels, the number and variety of species are indicated by the coloring. Pale shades of yellow represent those regions with few indigenous species, and the color deepens to strong orange where a great many species are found: the deeper the color, the greater the number of species in that area.

To facilitate identification of the individual genera, the entire plant is shown for orchids with flowers not bigger than an inch. Otherwise, the genus is depicted only by the flower, which is easily recognizable.

Spiranthes

Corallorhiza

Habenaria

Orchis

Cypripedium

Ondontoglossum

Epidendrum

Oncidium

Vanilla

Laelia

Cattleya

Catasetum

NORTH AMERICA

Catasetum

Ondontoglossum

Laelia

Vanilla

Epidendrum

Oncidium

Cattleya

Brassia

Coryanthes

Bulbophyllum

Spiranthes

Habenaria

SOUTH AMERICA

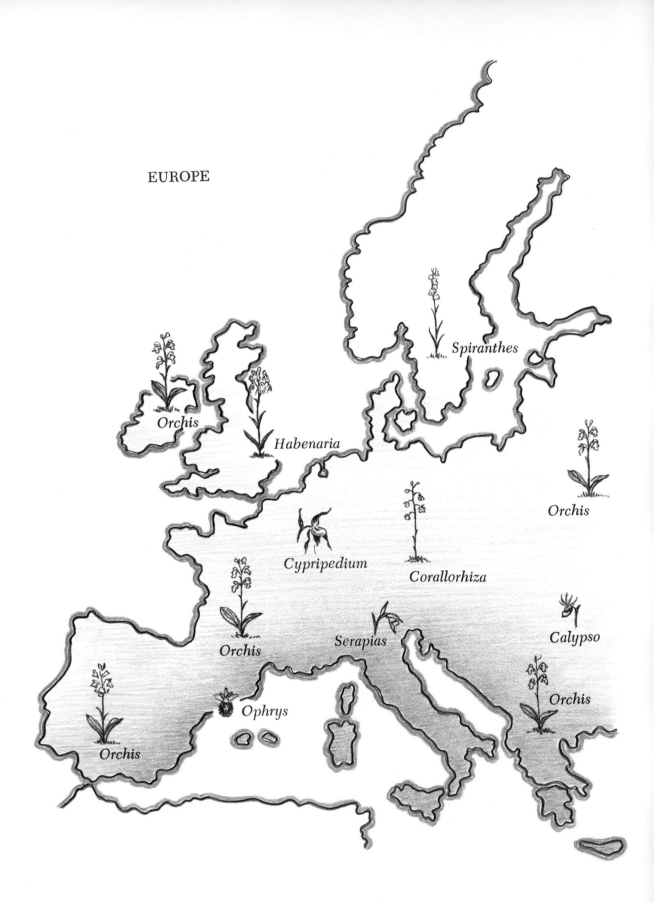

EUROPE

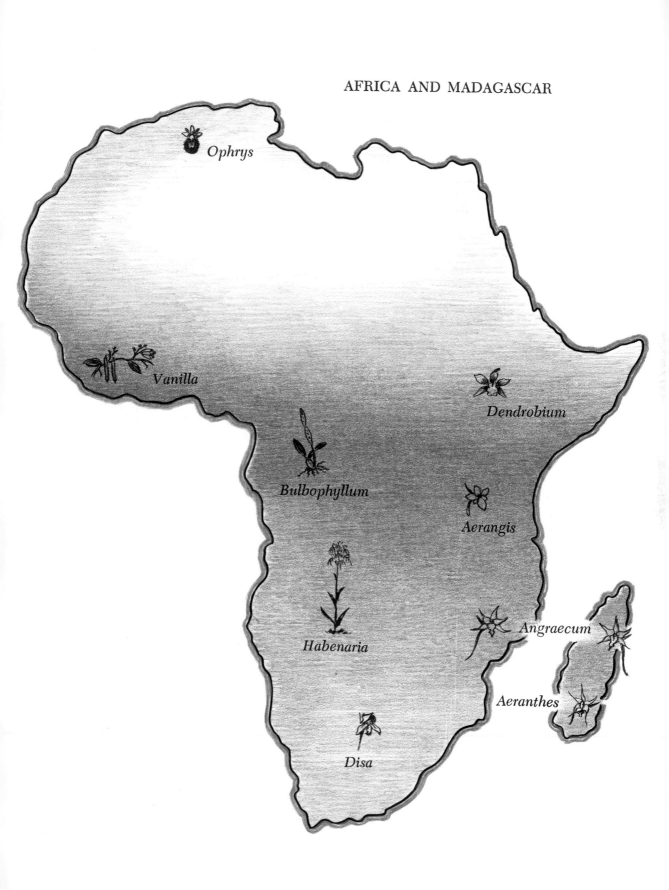

AFRICA AND MADAGASCAR

Ophrys

Vanilla

Dendrobium

Bulbophyllum

Aerangis

Habenaria

Angraecum

Aeranthes

Disa

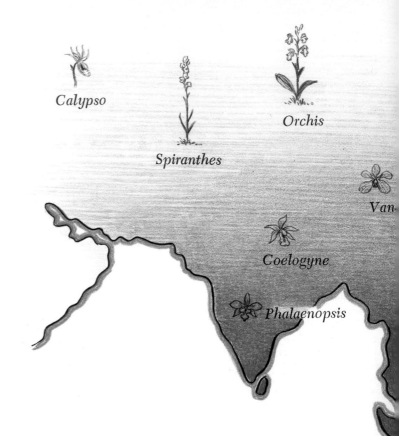

Calypso

Spiranthes

Orchis

Van-

Coelogyne

Phalaenopsis

Bulbophyll-

ASIA AND THE AUSTRO-MALAYAN REGION

Bibliography

Ayensu, Edward S. "Beautiful Gamblers of the Biosphere." *Natural History,* October 1974.

Corell, D. S. *Native Orchids of North America.* New York: Ronald Press, 1950.

Danesch, O. and E. "Orchids of the Species *Ophrys* in Majorca." Zeiss Information Bulletin No. 49.

Darwin, Charles. *The Various Contrivances by Which Orchids Are Fertilised by Insects.* 1862.

Dodson, C. H., and Gillespie, R. J. *Biology of the Orchids.* Mid-America Orchid Congress, 1967.

Janzen, D. H. "The Deflowering of Central America." *Natural History,* April 1974.

Kohlhaupt, P. *Bunte Welt der Orchideen.* Stuttgart: Franckh'sche Verlagshandlung, 1971.

Nebel, G. *Orchideen.* Gütersloh: C. Bertelsmann Verlag, 1958.

Ross, E. S. "Asian Insects in Disguise." *National Geographic,* September 1965.

Shuttleworth, F. S., and Zim, H. S. *Orchids.* New York: Golden Press, 1970.

Van der Pijl, L., and Dobson, C. H. *Orchid Flowers, Their Pollination and Evolution.* Coral Gables, Fla.: University of Miami Press, 1966.

Withner, C. L. *Orchids.* New York: Ronald Press, 1959.

Index

Page numbers in italics indicate illustrations.

Aceras anthropophora (Doll Orchid), 132, *132*
Aerangis, 96
Aerangis rhodostica, 96
Aeranthes, *96*
Aeranthes grandiflora, 97
Africa, 36, 88, 94–96, 118
  map, *151*
Alps, 21, 103, 104
Amazon River, 15
American Orchid Society, 16
Andes, 21, 76, 82
Angraecum, 94, 95
Antarctic region, 108
anther, 40, *41*, 42, 63, 66, 67
  of *Ornithocephalus*, 132
  of Trapdoor Orchid, *65*
ants, 78
Apennines, 104
aphrodisiacs, 20
Arctic region, 108
Argentina, 78, 84
Asia, 20, 88, 92, 94, 100, 114
  American orchids from, 121–23
  map, *152*
  miniature orchids of, 136–37
  See also specific countries
Australia, 64, 88, 92, 132, 133
  map, *153*

Bahamas, 121
Bamboo Orchid, 35–36, *36*, *37*
Bearded Orchid (*Pogonia ophioglossoides*), 121, *122*
Bee Orchid, *98*, *120*, 125, 127
bees, 56, 62, *62*, 104
  Catasetum and, *52*, 59–60, 63–64, 71
  color vision in, 58
  Ophrys and, 67–70, *68–69*, 127
  orchid mimicry of, 67, 69, 119, 125, *127*
  orchid traps for, 65–67
  See also smell
birds, 55, *55*, 58, 99, 132, *145*
  insect mimicry of, 127, 128
Bird's Nest Orchid (*Neottia nidus-avis*), 104–5, *105*

bisexual flowers, 38, *38*, 40–43, 45, 59, *59*
  self-pollination and, 53, 55
"black orchid," 28, 92
Black Orchid (*Coelogyne pandurata*), 91
Bletilla striata, 121, *122*
Bowerbird, Crestless Gardener, *145*
Braided Orchid (*Lockhartia,*), 140, *141*
Brassia longissima, 139, *139*
Brazil, 59, 78, 84, 99
Bucket Orchid, 64–65, *66*, *124*, 125, 131
Bulbophyllum, 60, *61*
Bulbophyllum longifolium, *30*
Bulbophyllum medusae, 139
Bumblebee Orchid, 127
bumblebees, 56
Burma, 88, 92
butterflies, 56, *56–57*, 118
  mimicry in, 127, *128*
Butterfly Orchid (*Oncidium papilio*), 87, *87*, 88, 125
Butterfly Orchid (*Orchis*), *115*
Butterfly Plant (*Phalaenopsis amabilis*), 92

Caladenia patersonii (Spider Orchid), 88, 125, 131
California, 94, 99
Calopogon, 121
Calopogon pulchellus (Grass Orchid), *121*
Calypso bulbosa, *113*
Calypso, 112, 114
Canada, 99, 100, 118
carbon dioxide, 78, 104
Catasetum, *52*, 58–60, 71
  sexual dimorphism of, *59*
  wishbone antennae in, *63*, 64
Cattley, James, 28
Cattleya, 16, *25*, 28–29, 74, *75*, 78–83, 84, 99
Cattleya bowringiana, 82
Cattleya forbesii, *81*
Cattleya gaskelliana, 79
Cattleya gigas, 79, 81
Cattleya guttata, 82, *82*

Cattleya rex, 82
Cattleya skinneri, 80
Cattleya violacea, 81
Central America, 70, 82, 99, 106, *148*
    See also specific countries
Chamaeorchis alpina, 104
China, 92, 118, 121, *152*
chlorophyll, 104, 106, 133
climate, 20–21, 28, 30, 76, 100
    adaptation to, 108–9, 118, 121, 123
Cockleshell Orchid (*Epidendrum coch-
    leatum*), 84, *84*, 99
Coelogyne, 91
Coelogyne cristata, 91, *91*
Coelogyne pandurata, 91
collecting, 14–15, 100, 112
color, 21, *26*, 66, 76
    "black species," 28, 91, 92
    blue rarities, *27*, *93*, 94, *95*
    insects and, 58, 59, 60
    range, in *Cattleya*, 81–82
    range, in *Dactylorhiza*, *116*, 118
    saprophytic orchids and, 104–7, 134
    temperate zone range of, 103
column, 38, 40, 45
    Bucket Orchid, *66*
    Trapdoor Orchid, *65*
Comparettia, 99
Corallorhiza, 105–6, *106*
Corallorhiza maculata, 106
Coryanthes, 64–65
Costa Rica, 60, 70
cotyledons, 33. *See also* leaves
Crestless Gardener Bowerbird, *145*
cross-pollination, *see* pollination
Cuba, 121, 143
Cucumber Orchid (*Dendrobium cucum-
    erinum*), 140, *140*
Cycnoches (Swan Orchids), *38*, 44–46,
    125, *126*, 131
Cycnoches chlorochilon, 44, *45*
Cymbidium, 92, 94
Cymbidium hookerianum, 94, *94*
Cypripedium (Lady's Slipper), *29*, 66–
    67, *109*, 131
    Fissipes, 112
    flowering age of, 50
    geographic range of, 109, 111–12
    Moccasin Flower, *110*, 111, 112
    Pink Lady's Slipper, *110*, 112
    popular names for, 111
    Showy Lady's Slipper, 112
    size range of, 136–37

Yellow Lady's Slipper, *110*, 112
    *See also Paphiopedilum; Phragmi-
    pedium caudatum*
Cypripedium calceolus, 111–12

Dactylorhiza, 116–18
Dactylorhiza majalis, 103
Dactylorhiza sambucina, *116*, 116–18
Dancing Ladies, 87
Darwin, Charles, 13–14, 44
    Catasetum and, 58–59, 64
Death's Head Moth, 125
Dendrobium, 75, 88–90, 140
Dendrobium cucumerinum (Cucumber
    Orchid), 140, *140*
Dendrobium fimbriatum, 90, *90*
Dendrobium formosum, 90
Dendrobium nobile, 90
Dendrobium phalaenopsis, 88, *144*, *145*
Dendrobium superbiens, 90
dicotyledons, 33
Dioscorides, Pedanius, 19
Disa, 94–95
Disa graminifolia, 95, *95*
Disa uniflora, 95
Doll Orchid (*Aceras anthropophora*),
    132, *132*
Dove Orchid (*Peristeria elata*), *131*, 132

ecological balance, 49, 70–71, 100, 109,
    112
embryo, *48*, 48–49
England, 14, 84
Epidendrum, 56–57, 84, 99
Epidendrum ciliare, 84
Epidendrum cochleatum (Cockleshell
    Orchid), 84, *84*, 99
epiphytic orchids, 15, 21, 30, *30*, 31, 75,
    99
    English first flowering, 84
    giant, 135–36
    leafless, 140–41
    pollination of, 44
    seeds of, 46–48
    water and, 76–78
Epipogium aphyllum (Glass Orchid),
    106–7, *107*
euglossid bees ("orchid bees"), *52*, 56,
    59–60, 71
Eurasia, 100, 111, 112, 115–16, 118
Europe, 19, 20, 99, 100, 103, *150*
    Aceras of, 132
    Lady's Slipper of, *109*, 111–12

orchid craze in, 14–15
Orchis of, 114, 115
saprophytes of, 104–6
See also specific countries

fertilizers, 49, 109
Fissipes, see Cypripedium
flies, 56, 60, 125
Flor de Jesus (*Laelia rubescens*), 83, *83*
Florida, 84, 99, 109, 121, 143, *148*
Fly Orchid, 125, 127
Flying-Bird Orchid, 125
Formosa, 91
France, 111
Frauenschuh, 111
funguses, 48–49, 104, 109

genera, 24. *See also specific genera*
Germany, 14, 111
Ghost Orchid (*Polyrrhiza lindenii*), *142*, 143
Glass Orchid (*Epipogium aphyllum*), 106–7, *107*
gnats, 56, 64
Gongora, 75
Gongora grossa, 66
Grammatophyllum, 135–36
Grammatophyllum speciosum, 135
Grass Orchid (*Calopogon pulchellus*), *121*
Greece, 19
Green Orchid (*Coelogyne pandurata*), 91
greenhouses, 14, 15, 24
growth patterns, 33–36, 133–43
Guatemala, 83, 86

Habenaria, 118
Habenaria ciliaris (Yellow Fringed Orchid), 118, *118*
Habenaria susannae, 118
Hammer Orchid, 132–33, *133*
Hawk Moths (Sphinx Moths), *12*, 14
Himalayas, 21, 35, 76, 88, 90, 91, 92
Holland, 14
Holy Ghost Orchid (*Peristeria elata*), *131*, 131–32
Humboldt, Alexander von, 112
hummingbirds, 55, 58, 99
hybridization, 16, 92
  natural, 24, 119
  Ophrys examples, *119*
hydathodes, 77

India, 91, 127, *152*
insecticides, 49
insects, 125
  in pollination, 13–14, 38, 42, 43, 44, 53, 55–71, 107, 118, *127*, 127–28, 132–33
  See also specific insects

Janzen, Daniel H., cited, 70–71
Japan, 92, 121

Knabenkraut, 20
Kohlröschen (*Nigritella*), 104

labellum, *see* lip (labellum)
Lady's Slipper, *see Cypripedium; Paphiopedilum; Phragmipedium Caudatum*
Laelia, *54*, 83
Laelia purpurata, 2
Laelia rubescens (Flor de Jesus), 83, *83*
laws, 100
Leaf Butterfly, 127, *128*
leaves, 21, 33, 35, 36, 38, 139–41
  Cattleya, *79, 80*
  of epiphytes, 77, 78, 136
  of saprophytes, 104, 106, 134
  temperate zone orchids, 100, 103, 111–12, 114
Lepanthopsis vinacea, 137
life span, 50–51
lip (labellum), 38, *39, 40, 41, 42, 43*, 94, 111
  of Bee Orchid, 127
  of *Calypso*, 114
  of *Cattleya*, 81, 82
  of *Coelogyne*, 91
  of *Cypripedium* (Lady's Slipper), 66, 111, 112
  of *Habenaria*, 118
  of Hammer Orchid, 132–33
  of *Orchis simia*, *114*, 115
  in pollination, 43–44, 64–65, 66–67, 69
  of *Vanda*, 92
Lockhartia, 140, *141*
Loroglossum hirzium, *40*

Madagascar, 13–14, 15, 28, 95, 96
  map, *151*
Majorca, 119
Malaysia, 28, 35, 118, 127, 130, 139
  map, *153*
mantis, 128, *129*, 130

maps, 147, *148–53*
Mask Orchid (*Aceras anthropophora*), 132
Maxillaria sophronitis, 137
medicine, 20
Mexico, 47, 51, 59, 78, 84, 99, *148*
Miami, Florida, 50
mimicry, 67, 69, 91, 119, 125–28
   insect use of, 128, 130
mineral salts, epiphytes and, 76–77
Minnesota, 112
Moccasin Flower, *110*, 111, 112
Monkey Orchid (*Orchis simia*), *114*, 115, 125
monkeys, 15
monocotyledons, 33
monopodial orchids, *32*, 33, 35
mosquitoes, 56, 64
Moth Orchid, 91–92, 125
moths, *13*, 13–14, 56, 58, 95, 118, 125, 143
mountain orchids, 103–4

Natural History (periodical), 70
nectar tubes, *see* spur
nectareaters, 55
nectary, *41*, 60–62, *62*
   Bird's Nest Orchid, 104
   Lady's Slipper, 67
   Star-of-Bethlehem Orchid, *12*, 13
Neottia nidus-avis, 104–5, *105*
New Guinea, 15, 91
New Zealand, map, *153*
Nigritella, 103–4
Nigritella nigra, *103*
Nodding Ladies' Tresses (*Spiranthes cernua*), 108–9
North Africa, 118, *151*
North America, 20, 99, 108–9, *148*
   Asian orchids in, 121–23
   Lady's Slipper of, 111, 112
   Orchis of, 114, 118
   saprophytes of, 105–6
Nova Scotia, 106, 109

Odontoglossum, 75, 84, 86
Odontoglossum crispum, 85, 86
Odontoglossum grande (Tiger Orchid), 86, *86*
odor, *see* smell
offshoots, 45, 55
Oncidium, 86–88, 137
Oncidium glossomystax, 137

Oncidium papilio (Butterfly Orchid), 87, *87*, 88
Ophrys, 67, *68–70*, 118–19, *120*
   mimicry in, 125–30, *127*
Ophrys apifera, 98
Ophrys bertolinii, 119
Ophrys hybrids, 119, *119*
Ophrys speculum, 119
Ophrys tenthredinifera, 119, *119*
Orchid Jungle, Miami, 50
Orchid Mantis, 128, *129*, 130
Orchid societies, 16, 100
Orchidaceae:
   insect mimicry of, 128, 130
   name origin, 17, 19–20
   See also specific genera and specific species
Orchis, 18, *19*, 19–20, *114*, 114–18, *115*
Orchis militaris, 114
Orchis morio, *101*
Orchis palustris, *102*, 103
Orchis purpurea, 115–16
Orchis simia (Monkey Orchid), 114, *114*, 115, 125
Orchis spectabilis (Showy Orchid), *117*, 118
Orinoco River, 15
Ornithocephalus, 132
Ornithocephalus bicornis, 140
ovary, 40, *42*, 43–44

Pacific Islands, map, *153*
Panama, 131
Paphinia grandiflora, 17
Paphiopedilum (Lady's Slipper), 88, 136–37
Paphiopedilum bellatulum (dwarf Lady's Slipper), *136*
Paphiopedilum insigne, 89
Peristeria elata (Holy Ghost or Dove Orchid), *131*, 131–32
Peru, 78, 82
petals, 24, 36, 38, *41*, 137
   Bucket Orchid, *66*
   Lady's Slipper, *138*
   Trapdoor Orchid, *65*
Phalaenopsis, 75, 91–92
Phalaenopsis amabilis, 72–73, 92
Phalaenopsis schilleriana, 92
Phalaenopsis stuartiana, 92
Philippines, 91
photosynthesis, 104, 106, 133
Phragmipedium caudatum, 137, *138*

Pink Lady's Slipper, *110*, 112
Pogonia ophioglossoides (Bearded Orchid), 121, *122*
pollen, *see* pollination; pollinium
pollination, 13–14, 38–43, 51, 52, *62*,
141–43
attraction mechanisms, 43–44, 53–71,
95, 104, 107, 119, 127–28, 131
birds in, *54–55*, 58, 99
butterflies in, *56–57*, *118*
repulsion mechanism, 132–33
self-pollination, 53, 55
pollinium, 40, *41*, 42, 43, 53, *62*, 65
Bucket Orchid, *66*
Catasetum, 63–64
glands of, 63
Polyrrhiza lindenii (Ghost Orchid), *142*,
143
propagation:
maturation time after, 49–51
vegetative, 45, 55
See also hybridization; pollination;
seeds
protocorm, *48*, 49
pseudobulbs, *34*, 35, 51, 77–78
size extremes, 135–36, 137
Pterostylis (Trapdoor Orchid), 64, *65*,
88, 125, 131
Punch-and-Judy Orchid, 125
Pyrenees, 104

resting periods, 51
Rhizanthella, 88, 133–34, *134*
rhizomes, 49
roots, *19*, 19–20, 100
Corallorhiza, 105–6, *106*
epiphytes and, 21, 30, 76, 78, 141
funguses and, 49
Ross, Edward S., 130
Royal Horticultural Society of England,
24
Russia, 111, 112

Salep, 20
saprophytic orchids, 104–7
subterranean, 21, 88, 133–34
scent, *see* smell
Scorpion Orchid, *130*, 131
seeds:
capsules, 32, 44, *45*, *46*
fungus symbiosis of, 48–49
Vanilla, *46*, 47–48
Selenipedium chica, 136

sepals, 24, 36, 38, *41*, 43, 139
Brassia longissima, *139*
Bucket Orchid, *66*
Calypso, 114
Cypripedium calceolus, 112
Disa, 94–95
Trapdoor Orchid, *65*
Serapias, 67
sex identification, 38, 59
shape, 21, *22–23*, 24, 28, 131–33
Epidendrum, 84
insect mimicry, 67, 69, 91, 119, 125–30
Lady's Slipper, *66*, 111
Orchis, 114–15
See also structure
Showy Lady's Slipper, 112
Showy Orchid (*Orchis spectabilis*), *117*,
118
size, 21, 28, 35–36, 78
Aeranthes, 96
giants, 24, *25*, 135–36
miniatures, 24, *24*, 136–37
Odontoglossum, 86
of temperate zone orchids, 100, 104,
115–16, 134
smell, 21, 28, 44, 76
insects' sense of, 58
pollination and, 38, 58–60, 66–67, 69,
95, 104, 107, 128
soil, 49, 76, 99, 103, 109, 133
Cypripedium and, 112
Sophronitis, 137
Sophronitis coccinea, 137
South Africa, 95, *151*
South America, 28, 86, 99, 137, *149*
orchid hunting in, 14–15
species, 15, 75, 78, 84, 119
classification criteria of, 33, 35, 38, 86
diversity of, 16–17, 19, 20, 21, 24, 28,
125
Habenaria distribution, 118
official count of, 24
tropical multiplication of, 99
See also specific species
Sphinx Moth (Hawk Moth), *13*, 14
Spider Orchid (*Caladenia patersonii*),
88, 125, 131
Spiranthes, 108–9
Spiranthes aestivalis, 108
Spiranthes cernua, 108–9
spur, 62, 107, 118, 141–43
Star-of-Bethlehem Orchid, *12*, 13–14
Stanhopea wardii, *50*, 51

Star-of-Bethlehem Orchid (*Angraecum*),
    12, 13–14, 95
stem, 24, 28, 36, 40, 44, 100
    of saprophytes, 104, 106, 107
    of sympodial orchids, 33, 35
    water conservation and, 77, 78
stigma, *41*, 42–43, 51, 53, *62*, 63, 64
    Bucket Orchid, *66*
    Trapdoor Orchid, *65*
structure, 17, 33–51
    parts, illustrated, *41*
    See also specific organs
subterranean orchids, 21, 88, 133, *134*
Swallowtail butterfly, *56–57*
Swamp Orchid (*Orchis palustris*), *102*,
    103
Swan Orchid (*Cycnoches*), 44–46, 125,
    126, 131
symbiosis, 48–49, 104, 109
sympodial orchids, 33, *34*, 35

Taiwan, 121
temperate zones, 19, 20, 30, 99–123
    bees of, 56, 67
    blooming times in, 51
    See also specific countries
Thailand, 88
Tiger Orchid (*Odontoglossum grande*),
    86, *86*
transplanting, 112
Trapdoor Orchid (*Pterostylis*), 64, *65*,
    88, 125, 131
trees: orchid growth in, 15, 21, 30, 135
    See also epiphytic orchids
Trichoglottis, 92
Trichoglottis philippinensis, 92
tropical zones, 14–15, 19, 20, 21, 28, 30,
    75–96, 99, 118
    bees of, 56

blooming times in, 51
    See also specific countries
tubers, *19*, 19–20, 49, 100, 114

United States of America, 84, 94, 99–
    100, 111, 123
    map, *148*
    See also specific states
Urals, 112

Vanda, 92
Vanda coerulea, 92, *93*
Vanda sanderiana, 92
Vanda teres, 92
Vanilla barbellata, 99
Vanilla, 20, 28, 47, 99
    seeds of, *46*, 47–48
Vanilla planifolia, 47
vanillin, 47
*Various Contrivances by Which Orchids
    Are Fertilised by Insects, The* (Dar-
    win), 14, 59

Walking Leaf Insect, 127
Wallace, Alfred Russel, 14
wasps, 56, 119
water:
    epiphytes and, 76–78
    saprophytes and, 104
    terrestrial orchids and, 103, 112
water orchids, 21
weed killers, 49

Yellow Fringed Orchid (*Habenaria
    ciliaris*), 118, *118*
Yellow Lady's Slipper, *110*, 112

Zeuxine strateumatica, 123